# Three American Moralists

## *Mailer, Bellow, Trilling*

Also by Nathan A. Scott, Jr.

*Rehearsals of Discomposure: Alienation and Reconciliation in Modern Literature* (1952)

*Modern Literature and the Religious Frontier* (1958)

*Albert Camus* (1962)

*Reinhold Niebuhr* (1963)

*Samuel Beckett* (1965)

*The Broken Center: Studies in the Theological Horizon of Modern Literature* (1966)

*Ernest Hemingway* (1966)

*Craters of the Spirit: Studies in the Modern Novel* (1968)

*Negative Capability: Studies in the New Literature and the Religious Situation* (1969)

*The Unquiet Vision: Mirrors of Man in Existentialism* (1969)

*Nathanael West* (1971)

*The Wild Prayer of Longing: Poetry and the Sacred* (1971)

Edited by Nathan A. Scott, Jr.

*The Tragic Vision and the Christian Faith* (1957)

*The New Orpheus: Essays toward a Christian Poetic* (1964)

*The Climate of Faith in Modern Literature* (1964)

*Man in the Modern Theatre* (1965)

*Four Ways of Modern Poetry* (1965)

*Forms of Extremity in the Modern Novel* (1965)

*The Modern Vision of Death* (1967)

*Adversity and Grace: Studies in Recent American Literature* (1968)

# Three American Moralists

## Mailer, Bellow, Trilling

Nathan A. Scott, Jr.

UNIVERSITY OF NOTRE DAME PRESS
NOTRE DAME          LONDON

Copyright © 1973 by
University of Notre Dame Press
Notre Dame, Indiana 46556

Library of Congress Cataloging in Publication Date

Scott, Nathan A
    Three American moralists.

    Includes bibliographical references.
    1. Mailer, Norman. 2. Bellow, Saul. 3. Trilling,
Lionel, 1905-      I. Title.
PS221.533      813'.03      73-11558
ISBN 0-268-00504-4
ISBN 0-268-00507-9 (pbk.)

Manufactured in the United States of America

*To*

Erich Heller

*and to*

Mircea and Christinel Eliade

# Contents

# Introduction

# Introduction

The *Kulturkampf* that has lain so heavily on the American scene since the early 1960s may now seem to situate what is called the New Sensibility at a considerable remove from the dim, gray years of the Eisenhower dispensation. Indeed, those of us who had reached adulthood at least by the close of the Second World War will surely feel today a very great difference of tone and atmosphere between that earlier period and the present time. For, then, the intellectual community had already deeply absorbed the lessons of F. O. Matthiessen and Perry Miller and Reinhold Niebuhr and Lionel Trilling and various others about what was beginning to be called "the American imagination." And it was coming to be assumed that the American mode of imagination was one which found its most natural standpoint in an essentially melodramatic view of human experience. Ours, we had decided, is a tradition whose most deeply ingrained habit has been—from Jonathan Edwards to Henry James and from Herman Melville to William Faulkner—to conceive the human story as an affair of great clashing contraries, as an infuriate struggle between the Legions of Light and the Hosts of Darkness. Indeed, remembering (as we had been taught to do by the new specialists in American Studies) the line of Poe, Hawthorne, Melville, Henry Adams, and Mark Twain, we were disposed to locate the place normally indwelt by the American mind not amongst any "temperate zones" but amongst what Emerson called "the extremities and suburbs" of the world. "Do I contradict myself/Very well then I contradict myself," Whitman had said. And the sanguinity of his admission seemed to make a kind of emblem of a native bias that had persistently been drawn to extravagant oppositions and stark dualities, whether in the form of the Calvinism of the New England Puritans or the "Manichaean" radicalism of our most characteristic literature or the oscillations of our politics between nostalgia and utopianism.

By the time of the early fifties, however, we had settled deeply into the straits of our struggle with the powers behind the Iron Curtain, and the bitter dilemmas of that engagement appeared no longer to permit any indulgence of our national penchant for contrariety. Indeed, all counsels of prudence seemed to recommend that the national imagination carefully accommodate its old enchantment with turmoil and conflict to the difficult exigencies of the Cold War. For, in these latter days of our distress, the issues of ambiguity and paradox had suddenly taken on a new moral prestige, and politics thus became a gesture in the direction of "the tragic sense of life."

Van Wyck Brooks—the Brooks of *America's Coming of Age* (1915)—had long since forfeited his earlier eminence as a result of what was felt to be the essentially retrogressive and sterile piety toward the American past expressed in his great multivolume project on "the literary life in America," *Makers and Finders.* Yet, strangely, it was Brooks's program for dealing with the contradiction and anomaly of American experience that was by way of being generally adopted by intellectuals in this country twenty years ago. For what he had proposed in *America's Coming*

*of Age* was that the extremes of thought and feeling
endemic to our culture be assuaged by such an "open,
skeptical, sympathetic centrality" as would provide "a
certain focal center" or "national 'point of rest' " wherein
extremities and contradictions could be so modulated as to
become endurable. And, despite the loss of celebrity that
Brooks had suffered during the generation that had inter-
vened since his brilliant book of 1915, it was something
very much like his stoical program of moderation that
became a prevailing creed among liberal intellectuals in the
postwar period of the late forties and early fifties: the
major platform of the time was established by the myth of
what Arthur Schlesinger, Jr., called "the vital center."[1]

It was undoubtedly this new "skeptical . . . centrality,"
with its yearning for a "national 'point of rest,' " that
prompted the intellectual community in these years to
find the public presence of Adlai Stevenson so enormously
engaging. Irving Howe's reconstruction of the matter is
wonderfully exact when he suggests that Stevenson's ap-
peal for intellectuals at the beginning of the 1950s was
largely rooted in the fact that, though they had been
singed just enough by the alliances with Stalinism in the
thirties and forties to want now to avoid any great cru-
sades, they

> . . . still enjoyed a mild idealistic lilt; they were tempted
> to abandon politics entirely yet felt themselves forced—
> indeed, trapped—into a lukewarm, gingerly participa-
> tion; they wished for liberal humaneness but felt that to
> identify with any social class or group was outmoded,
> deficient in tone. And here was this remarkable man
> from Illinois, so charming and cultivated, so witty and

[1]See Arthur M. Schlesinger, Jr., *The Vital Center: The Politics of
Freedom* (Boston: Houghton Mifflin Co., 1949).

so . . . well, *somewhat* weary . . . come to represent and speak for them.[2]

Which is to say that Stevenson's very distaste for politics (at least as the tone of his public deliverances made it seem) made him appear a kind of "emblem of the intellectual condition"[3] and thus one to be identified with and admired. He did, of course, command an immense distinction as an American public man wholly committed to those modes of discourse appropriate to freemen. But his characteristic style—in its air of fastidious ambivalence before the messiness of political actuality—did, indeed, have the effect of confirming a similar ambivalence that had come to be deeply a part of "the liberal imagination." For, as Lionel Trilling was eloquently contending in much of his critical work of this period, after all the expensive disorders of the first half of the twentieth century, the great secret hope of the liberal intelligence was often a hope "that man's life in politics, which is to say, man's life in history, shall come to an end."[4] And he suggested that the "growing estrangement from history"[5] deserved to be considered a sign of desperation.

Now the idiom and tone of American cultural life today entail styles radically different from those which were prevailing twenty years ago. For the emphasis then on the necessity of achieving flexibility and modulation, of carefully keeping (as Mr. Trilling phrased it) an awareness of "variousness and possibility, . . . of complexity and difficulty,"[6] will seem from our present vantage point to have

[2]Irving Howe, *Steady Work: Essays in the Politics of Democratic Radicalism* (New York: Harcourt, Brace & World, 1966), p. 207.

[3]*Ibid.*, p. 209.

[4]Lionel Trilling, *The Liberal Imagination* (New York: Viking Press, 1950), p. 195.

[5]*Ibid.*, p. 196.

[6]*Ibid.*, p. xv.

thrown an odd sort of mutedness and quiet over cultural life, and to have sponsored such a retreat from social reality as made for a general muffling of any sound of combat. Whereas today, after the jackhammer barrage of the past few years—of psychedelic discothéques and high-decibel Rock, of "multimedia" Events and electronic Happenings, of terrorist assaults on our universities and holocausts in our cities, and of the endless "offensives" conducted by the choreographers of "confrontation politics"—we have a sense of belonging to the noisiest period of this century; and certainly the din of the New Sensibility will seem to place it at a great distance from the styles of thought and feeling which were predominant two decades ago. But beneath all the shrillness and bedlam and amidst all the rampant apocalypticism, it just may be possible to detect a secret hope not unlike that of an earlier time—that we may somehow find a way of releasing ourselves altogether from the duties and contingencies of our life in history.

The weathers of our culture have been lately harsh, too exigent indeed for comfort of spirit; and only the blind and the callous can be unembarrassed by the squalor that today disfigures much of the social and political fabric of American life. The terrible netherworld of the black urban ghettos, the immense and stubbornly self-perpetuating poverty across the land, the stupid inertia and mediocrity of our governmental bureaucracies, the muck and mess and fumes that contaminate our great cities—in all this and more, any movement of dissent today can easily find its enabling charter. But what is striking about the "mystical militancy" (as Michael Harrington has phrased it[7]) of much recent radical protest is not that it should have pronounced a word of severe judgment but that it should

[7]See Michael Harrington, "The Mystical Militants," *The New Republic*, 19 February 1966: pp. 20-22.

so frequently have been ruled by a mood of eschatological excitement, by a sense of the present age as a time approaching the end-point of its course, when we are at the edge of some great cliff. As this attitude is translated into manners, morals, and politics, the anonymous voice that begins to be heard is very much like that voice which is repeatedly heard in the section of *The Waste Land* called "A Game of Chess," where the Cockneys Bill and Lou and May are foregathered in some London pub whose proprietor, being eager to close up for the night, keeps saying, "HURRY UP PLEASE ITS TIME." Hurry up, please: it's time—time, that is, for some great leap (over the cliff's edge perhaps), for ours is an extreme situation. It is just such an urgent and ominous cry that we have constantly heard amidst much of the furious skirmishing that has disrupted the American scene in recent years—hurry up, please: it's time!

Apocalypticism, as a distinctive way of managing reality, is, of course, a method which the imagination tends to employ precisely in those moments when the realities of history seem to be quite unmanageable. As with ancient Jewish apocalypticism, so with all subsequent outbursts of apocalyptic hysteria: the convulsive embrace of some vision of the End has been prompted by a sense of the utter intolerableness of historical actuality. Zion has been destroyed, Babylon has been spared: there ensues a great collapse of confidence in the possibility of history taking any new and more hopeful direction. So the apocalyptist, finding the world in its present form unendurable, proposes, with a certain heroic gesture, a sort of *amor fati* as the way out. The "radically demanding historical hour"[8] being intolerable, he looks toward the time when time shall be no more, when the world in which the Chosen

[8]Martin Buber, *Pointing the Way*, trans. by Maurice Friedman (New York: Harper & Bros., 1957), p. 203.

People are so cruelly disadvantaged will have been replaced by a New Jerusalem. In short, his resistance to history, his eagerness to get out of it altogether, is his way of dealing with a history felt to be no longer manageable.

And ours is in many ways an age which is a very bad time indeed. But the times of human life perhaps are always difficult. Brightness is often fallen from the skies; and the nonchalance wherewith in the daily round we are enabled, nevertheless, to get on with the conduct of life is no doubt very largely an affair of what Paul Tillich spoke of as·"the courage to be."[9] Indeed, the bewitching glamor of Apocalypse today suggests that recovering the courage-to-be may present the most fundamental of all the various hard imperatives confronting the spirituality of our period. For what is always betokened by an apocalyptic insurgency is a failure of courage, of the kind of courage that permits us to reckon with the conditioned and imperfect reality of ourselves and the world to which we are committed by the logic of our history. And when this most elemental of virtues is lost, the great summons that beckons is one which invites us to seek again for the grounds on which we may repose some confidence in the possibility of our finding the world, unsatisfactory as it is, a place wherein we may undertake to do battle with Moloch and whomever or whatever else it may be that threatens our commitment to the human enterprise of dwelling in historical time.

Many of the most prestigious agencies of the cultural imagination in America today would, of course, encourage us to slouch—or to dash—toward a New Jerusalem. Nor is our literature untouched by the passion for millenialist ecstasy, for Paradise Now. Yet the literary intelligence of the present time, when it is most vital, often has it as a

[9]See Paul Tillich, *The Courage to Be* (New Haven: Yale University Press, 1952).

part of its genius to urge, in effect, some reappraisal of the recently influential assumption that it is our duty to hurry along toward that "Sabbath of Eternity . . . when time no more shall be."[10] And the three writers whose testimony is brought under review in the following pages (the novelists Norman Mailer and Saul Bellow, and the novelist-critic Lionel Trilling) are, in their extreme diversity and strange likeness, marvelously exemplary figures. They are Jews—and thoroughly secular men. But though they find grace and glory not in infinites and eternities but in the quotidian realities that are at hand for the creatures of this world, neither wants (not even Mr. Trilling) simply to elect

> the moderate Aristotelian city
> Of darning and the Eight-Fifteen, where Euclid's geometry
> And Newton's mechanics would account for our experience,
> And the kitchen table exists because I scrub it.[11]

Indeed, far from seeming to be among Blake's horses of instruction, Norman Mailer at least (by way of the *persona* he has craftily fixed in the minds of his contemporaries) will doubtless appear to belong among those tigers of wrath whose intention it is to scare us off the established roads of our common journey. Nor do Bellow and Trilling, for all of their unillusioned knowledge of "the foul rag-and-bone shop of the heart," want to speak any word against life in the heroic mode, against boldness and energy and *esprit*. Yet, though they propose different forms of courage as normative for the human venture, neither permits his vision of the extremest boundaries of the world to

[10]Norman O. Brown, *Life Against Death: The Psychoanalytical Meaning of History* (Middletown, Conn.: Wesleyan University Press, 1959), p. 93.
[11]W. H. Auden, "For the Time Being: A Christmas Oratorio," in his *Collected Poetry* (New York: Random House, 1945), p. 465.

overrule his sense of man's being unable to get anywhere
except by way of a path that leads *through* the concrete
materialities of his condition. Not even Norman Mailer, for
all of his commitment to an "existential" ethic, supposes
that by any feat of sheer will we can simply burst the belt
and win through to the unhistorical realm of the Heavenly
City. They take it for granted that (as the old maxim of
Heraclitus puts it) "the way up is the way down," that the
way towards fullness of being leads descendingly through
the whole actuality of our creaturely life. And the large
confidence they express (through radically different idi-
oms) in the strength of the human thing gives them the
status of public moralists in a period when, as it would
seem, so many harbor the gravest doubts about the capacity of man to survive the stringencies of historical time.

Norman Mailer, Saul Bellow, Lionel Trilling: these three
may be said—without reference to the momentary fluctua-
tions of the cultural stock market—to be at the absolute
center of what is most deeply animating in American
literature of the present and the recent past. There is much
else, of course, that has enormous interest and value and
much that these three figures cannot be said, in and of
themselves, to embody. But they are surely among the
major bench marks of our period. They mirror the age in
the modes of their response to

this iron time
Of doubts, disputes, distractions, fears.[12]

They offer, though, not only a mirror of the age but also,
from quite various perspectives, a releasing view of the
stoutness of the human spirit; and it is that view which it is
the purpose of this little book to scan.

---

[12]Matthew Arnold, "Memorial Verses," in his *Poetical Works* (London: Macmillan & Co., 1901), p. 290.

# Norman Mailer - Our Whitman

# II

# Norman Mailer - Our Whitman

*Brood on that country who expresses our will.*
*She is America. . . .*
                    —The Armies of the Night

*O what am I that I should not seem*
*For the song's sake a fool!*
                    —William Butler Yeats, "A Prayer
                              for Old Age"

It is a convention among students of Kierkegaard, as they refer to the *oeuvre* which is at once their delight and their burden, to speak of it as "Kierkegaard's literature." And, in declaring the work of this astonishing Danish prodigy to be indeed a "literature," this usage intends to speak not only of its massiveness of size but also of its electrifying variousness of idiom and of the extraordinary diversity of authorial persona which it reflects. To attempt any serious engagement with the intelligence that created such works as *The Sickness unto Death* and the *Concluding Unscientific Postscript* and *Either/Or* is to find oneself dealing with a personality marvelously capacious and fertile and protean, so much so that it seems to surpass every neat conceptual chart—and the richness of the legacy is felt, therefore, to represent an achievement that must be

15

thought of as constituting a veritable *literature*. And so it is with the writer whose career is presently felt to be more thrusting and imperative than any other on the American scene of the 1970s. The weight and substance of Norman Mailer's thought, we can be certain, make his merit radically incommensurable with Kierkegaard's. Among his novels, he has produced no single work that approximates the brilliance of Saul Bellow's *Seize the Day* or the sagacity of Bellow's *Mr. Sammler's Planet* or the unmistakable eminence of Ellison's *Invisible Man*. But the singular bravura and the stunning multifariousness of strategem with which Mailer has proceeded to explore and dramatize the stricken years through which we have moved since the time of the Second World War make his the most vivid image in American literary life today; and the unexampled versatility of his performance as a writer gives us now a sense not only of his *oeuvre* being harder to judge than that of any other American writer of his generation but of its making a sort of "literature" outside the usual categories of appraisal that we apply either to fiction or to journalism.

Indeed, it would not be wholly incomprehensible were the search for some metric appropriate to Norman Mailer's special presence today in the national forum to result in his being thought of as *our* Whitman. In one of the most memorable passages of *American Renaissance*, F. O. Matthiessen spoke of Whitman as one who (along with Melville and Thoreau) strove for a "likeness of 'man in the open air' "[1]—whereas Mailer's scene is frequently (as in *Barbary Shore* and *The Deer Park* and *An American Dream*) some enclosed and airless (as he would say, even "funky") room unadjusted either to the sun by day or the stars by night. Nor does his devotion to an "existential politics . . . rooted

[1]See F. O. Matthiessen, *American Renaissance: Art and Expression in the Age of Emerson and Whitman* (New York: Oxford University Press, 1941), p. 635.

in the concept of the hero" find any antecedent in Whitman, who was prepared to admit (as he said in *Democratic Vistas*) that the generality of humankind "is full of vulgar contradictions and offense" but who nevertheless believed that "always waiting untold in the souls of the armies of common people, is stuff better than anything that can possibly appear in the leadership of the same." And the insistently celebratory note being struck a hundred years ago by the great *Meistersinger* of *Leaves of Grass* may seem to be sharply contravened by the aggressively polemical tone of *The Deer Park* and *The Presidential Papers*. Furthermore, there is much in the quirkiness of Mailer's moral style that Whitman would no doubt have found distressing and even monstrous—most assuredly, for example, the desire being professed in *Advertisements for Myself* to enter into "the mysteries of murder, suicide, incest, orgy, orgasm, and Time." In this connection, it may also be remarked that Mailer would very probably be at least slightly nettled by any juxtoposition of himself with Whitman, largely by reason of the contradiction in sexual ideology between his own highly assertive heterosexuality and Whitman's implicit homosexualism.

But after all sorts of large and obvious divergences have been totted up, there remain many impressive parallels between these two exemplary poets of life in the United States, and parallels sufficiently substantial to make their notation a way of beginning to draw a circle of definition about the figure whose testimony is perhaps more filled with challenge than that of any other writer in the American literary life of our period. Both embrace, of course, a notable multiplicity of roles—Whitman as Brooklyn dandy and sexual liberator, as friend and comforter to maimed veterans of the Civil War in Washington hospitals, as national Bard and the Good Gray Poet; Mailer as Reichian eschatologist and self-appointed counselor to the White

House, as apostle of Hipsterism and New York mayoralty
candidate, as guru to the nonparticipants and dropouts and
chief jester to the WASP Mafia on the Main Streets of
America, as practitioner of an increasingly idiosyncratic
novelistic art, and as the most consummately gifted journalist of our time. And, like the "camerado" of *Leaves of
Grass*, Mailer is

> one of the roughs, a kosmos,
> Disorderly fleshy and sensual . . . eating drinking and
>     breeding,
> No sentimentalist . . . no stander above men and women or
>     apart from them . . . no more modest than immodest.

But neither of these "roughs" is a simple man: both
present, in personality, a strange admixture of gaiety and
neuroticism, of insouciance and combativeness—though,
finally, the impression conveyed is that of a most exuberant egotism. Yet it is not an egotism so imperious as to
convert their art into an exercise in narcissism, for, with
both, the literary project is radically committed to a rendering of the American reality. Mailer, too, one feels, takes
it for granted (as Whitman said in the Preface he prepared
for the 1855 edition of *Leaves of Grass*) that "The United
States themselves are essentially the greatest poem." And
believing that the writer must be, in Whitman's phrase,
"commensurate with the people," he has undertaken
(again, in the language with which Whitman's 1855 Preface
speaks of the poet's obligation) to "flood himself with the
immediate age as with vast oceanic tides." Which is why
his art is a vernacular art, often ranged (like Whitman's)—as
in, say, the extraordinary novel of 1967, *Why Are We in
Vietnam?*—in a kind of middle region between lyric poetry
and prose narrative. And since his dedication to the actuality of "the immediate age" requires him to try to be a
seismograph of the deepest tremors of our national spirit—

or a "mirror carried through the streets"[2]—Mailer constantly keeps, for all his literary virtuosity, a certain mistrust of belles-lettres, so that one can easily imagine him being prepared to make an avowal something like that which occurs in Whitman's essay of 1888, "A Backward Glance O'er Travel'd Roads," that "No one will get at my verses who insists upon viewing them as a literary performance, or attempt at such performance, or as aiming mainly toward art or aestheticism."

Nor are the affinities between Mailer and Whitman limited to matters of personal style and the general slant of their careers: they are also affinities more substantive, involving numerous striking coincidences of basic emphasis and concern. We will, for example, readily recall the asperity with which the Whitman of *Democratic Vistas* faced the new American scene that had begun to emerge after the close of the Civil War. The increasing preoccupation of his fellow countrymen with "flesh, incomes . . . merchandise . . . solid perpetuities, buildings of brick and iron" represented for him nothing more than a rampant philistinism, and thus he had no hesitancy in declaring:

> Never was there, perhaps, more hollowness at heart than at present, and here in the United States. Genuine belief seems to have left us. The underlying principles of the States are not honestly believ'd in (for all this hectic glow, and these melodramatic screamings), nor is humanity itself believ'd in. What penetrating eye does not everywhere see through the mask? The spectacle is appalling. We live in an atmosphere of hypocrisy throughout. . . . The depravity of the business classes of our country is not less than has been supposed, but infinitely greater. The official services of America, national,

[2]Ralph Waldo Emerson, *The Complete Works*, 12 vols. (Boston: Houghton Mifflin Co., 1903-4), III, p. 41.

state, and municipal, in all their branches and depart-
ments, except the judiciary, are saturated in corruption,
bribery, falsehood, maladministration; and the judiciary
is tainted. The great cities reek with respectable as much
as nonrespectable robbery and scoundrelism. In fashionable life, flippancy, tepid amours, weak infidelism, small
aims, or no aims at all, only to kill time. . . . In vain have
we annex'd Texas, California, Alaska, and reach north
for Canada and south for Cuba. It is as if we were
somehow being endow'd with a vast and more and more
thoroughly appointed body, and then left with little or
no soul.

Such an indictment and such a warning were frequently
the burden of Whitman's message in his last years. But it is
not to be forgotten that this strain in *Democratic Vistas* is
by no means absent from the poetic formulations presented in *Leaves of Grass*, for there, too, he is often to be
found voicing a very stringent judgment of the American
character—as when, for example, in "Song of the Open
Road" (1856) he expresses his chagrin at how much the
typical American begins to be not a simple, separate self
but a self which is only
    a duplicate of every one, skulking and hiding it goes,
Formless and wordless through the streets of the cities,
        polite and bland in the parlors,
In the cars of railroads, in steamboats, in the public as-
        sembly . . .
Smartly attired, countenance smiling, form upright, death
        under the breast-bones, hell under the skullbones . . .
Keeping fair with the customs, speaking not a syllable of
        itself,
Speaking of any thing else but never of itself.

Now the Whitman whose dismay at the America of
Buchanan and Fillmore and Grant led him to call most

urgently for "more compaction and more moral identity"
is not at all distant from the Mailer who, over these past
years, has raged against the slummy wilderness of his
country's contriving—with its raped landscape, its bleak
new architecture, its dehumanizing technocracy, its sexual
repression and "tepid amours," its addiction to drugs and
contraceptives and plastics, its penchant for foods poi-
soned by chemical additives, and its ungovernable social-
political violence. Here, as he wants to say, in this fearfully
injured land, we suffer "some unendurable stricture of
eternity" whose sign (in his mythology) is our astonishing
susceptibility to cancer. To the world of "urban renewal,
mental hygiene, [and] the wave of the waveless future" he
(to adopt the great negative attributed by Melville to
Hawthorne) is prepared to say "No! in thunder." And, like
Whitman, he reposes no great faith in any particular
scheme of social reorganization or political reform, believing (with the author of *Democratic Vistas*) that the re-
humanizing of American society awaits a profoundly spiritual regeneration—"more compaction and more moral
identity." As the poet of "When Lilacs Last in the Door-
yard Bloom'd" felt that Lincoln, in the nobility of his own
person, had held forth an enormous promise to America,
so the author of *The Presidential Papers* felt that in John
Kennedy had come the chance for a great new beginning.
But Mailer's most fundamental commitment is not to the
politics of social reconstruction but to the politics of
salvation, and the course that he plots runs closely parallel
to that of his great nineteenth-century progenitor. For he
is convinced that our health and peace are at last to be
found only in a recovery of what the "Song of Myself"
speaks of as "Nature without check with original energy."
And it is his passionate quest of this *justitia originalis* that
prompts him—like that earlier Dionysiac who wanted to
unscrew all the locks from all the doors and "the doors

themselves from their jambs"—to undertake an allegiance to dark powers and phallic deities. Indeed, ever since his famous manifesto of 1957, "The White Negro," the soteriology that Mailer has been recommending would seem to have had as a major premise the doctrine of a sort of *via negativa*, the notion that a descent into hazard and darkness must precede any renewal of the heart or renovation of the commonweal. He tells us that "slack diseases, featureless, symptomless diseases like virus and colds and the ubiquitous cancer are the appropriate metaphor" and the sure sign of the special rottenness that poisons American culture today. But a crucial line in his Preface to *The Presidential Papers* says: "Acute disease is cure." He reasons:

> When the body is sick, it is usually because one or another organ has become too weak or too powerful in its function. If the disproportion is acute, a war goes on in the body, an inflammatory sickness, a fever, a crisis. The war decided, the organ subsides, different in size, stronger or weaker, it returns to its part of the body's function. Acute disease is cure.

It is in fact his homeopathic devotion to the ancient law *similia similibus curantur* ("like is cured by like") which is at the bottom of his much flourished "existentialism," for about all Mailer means by this term is living dangerously, dangerously enough to permit the disease to become acute—and thus to cure. And the man who recklessly speaks of death as the "existential continuation of life" is, again, not far removed from the Whitman who wanted to create a poetry affirmative not only of life but also of "merging! And Death!" and who, in "Scented Herbage" (1860), spoke of its having been "convey'd" to him that death—by which he meant the *askésis* of heartache and suffering—is "the real reality."

So, brooding on the American soulscape—as he has done over the past two decades, with an intensity and an eloquence and an incautiousness that make him one of the great marvels of our time—Norman Mailer may well indeed deserve to be considered in these late years *our* Whitman.

\*      \*      \*

The amazingly precocious performance, *The Naked and the Dead*, which established Mailer in 1948, at the age of twenty-five, as a major presence in our literary life was a novel ostensibly devoted to the Pacific theatre of the Second World War. It may at first seem a little absurd to speak of a novel so drenched in the experience of that whole adventure as one which deals with it only ostensibly. Certainly the thousands of people who bought copies of the early editions and the thousands more who have continued to purchase cheap reprints are people who have been drawn to the book chiefly by its brilliantly executed and moving evocations of what it was like for GIs in the American infantry to pursue an elusive enemy through the stifling heat and foul air and across the treacherous swamps and slopes of a jungle in the Pacific. And, on this level, it does, of course, constitute the most impressive document that any writer of Mailer's generation produced of American military experience during the crisis of the 1940s. But, for all the skillfulness with which the novel, in its craft, was deploying the strategies of naturalistic fiction descending most immediately from Dos Passos and Farrell and Steinbeck, it lacks any significant technical interest of an innovative sort; and, were the range of its implication restricted to the actions and occasions of the Second World War, it would doubtless by now have slipped into the obscurity which has overtaken that fictional reportage on the wartime emergencies of those years represented by novels such as Alfred Hayes's *All Thy Conquests* (1946) and Gore Vidal's *Williwaw* (1946), or by Harry Brown's *A Walk in the Sun* (1944) and James Jones's *From Here to Eternity* (1951). Yet, unlike that large body of fiction which found its materials in the drama of World War II, *The Naked and the Dead* remains today a stubbornly commanding book; and it does so, in part, because, beneath its ostensible engagement with the transitory circumstances of the war years, it is advancing a powerfully negative assessment of the essential health of American society.

The chief vehicle of Mailer's analysis was the device of the "Time Machine,"[3] which is the novel's designation for those long flashbacks over the formative circumstances out of which each of the principal characters had come before being drawn up into the action of the war. There is Gallagher, a Jew-baiting little Irishman, whose face slants "resentfully to one side" and who always appears "wroth"—a man out of the gray slums of Boston's Roxbury district whose teachers never remembered him in high school; who has drifted from one menial job to another, glad to be a flunky for the Democratic Club in his ward as he hopes for some minor bit of patronage; wishing, whenever at night he looks across the Charles River at the lighted Harvard campus, that somebody would "wipe out all those mother-fuggers"; weary of his whining drone of a wife; and forever filled with murderous angers, as he slouches through a world in which he is in every way unequipped to reach any sort of security or fulfillment. Or there is the tall, bony vagabond from the hills of Montana, Red Valsen, whose "profile consisted almost entirely of a

[3]This mechanism was obviously derived, as a narrative procedure, from the "biographies" of Dos Passos's *U.S.A.* trilogy and, in its nomenclature, from Dos Passos's "Newsreels" and "Camera Eyes."

large blob of a nose and a long low-slung jaw, a combination which made his face seem boiled and angry"—support-
ing his family at the age of thirteen after his father's death
in a mine shaft explosion; leaving home at eighteen because he doesn't want to "sweat out his guts" in a coal
mine, and thereafter wandering across the country, living
in cheap rooming houses, and working as dishwasher or
short-order cook or farmhand, but always moving on—
volunteering for military service finally because "in the
war you keep on moving." Or there is the Mexican boy
from the slums of San Antonio, Julio Martinez, who loves
to think of himself as a "Texan" but who has never so
designated himself because, always, he keeps deep in his
mind images of "the tall white men with the slow voices
and the cold eyes," and he is fearful of the look that might
appear on these faces were he to say "Martinez is a
Texan"—a slim, graceful, intelligent lad who has forever
breathed the American fables about "heroes, aviators, lovers, financiers" and who is drunk with the American dream
but forever shut out of the white man's world. Then there
is Sam Croft (of whom his father once said, "Well, now,
my Sam is a mean boy. I reckon he was whelped
mean.")—like Martinez out of Texas, but from the state's
western desert region; a man whose education was an affair
of deer hunting and busting horses and of the coarse,
violent talk in bunkhouses about niggers and "nookie" and
"whoors"; a man with "a crude unformed vision in his
soul ... [of which] he was rarely conscious," who wants
no buddy and who is "stirred with an odd ecstasy" before
he fires a gun. And, along with these, the particular infantry group forming the novel's main cast of characters
includes the sturdy young Jew from Brooklyn, Joey Gold-
stein, hardworking graduate of a welding school, eager and
ambitious, with extra money coming in from overtime and
just beginning to prosper a little when he is drafted in

1943, but whose empty and joyless marriage has often brought him close to hysteria and terror; or there is Roth, the timid, plaintive graduate of C.C.N.Y. so pathetically proud of his thin, vague culture; and Brown, the bumptious middle-class salesman whose one great certitude is that women will "cheat on ya even when you do give 'em something to remember"—and various others all moved by some great pain shaped by the hard, brutal world of which they as Americans are exhibited as representative types.

Indeed, in the logic of the novel, it is the function of the Army, in the harshness of its authoritarianism and indifference to the individual person, to be the very simulacrum of the society which produces the kinds of human malformations embodied in these men. Thus a central figure in Mailer's design is General Cummings. For he heads the division which has invaded the Pacific island of Anopopei, where the action of the novel's primary narrative line takes place. And he is a monster—a superbly gifted administrator and military tactician with some capacity for sustained reflection on his experience at a high level of generality, but one who is so much a sensualist of power as to be, in the nakedest way, an absolute *exemplum* of the corrosive inhumanity belonging to a culture fallen under the sway of the *désacralisé*. Though as an American soldier he is engaged in a war against the forces of totalitarianism, he does in fact consider the ultimate political truth to be resident in that calculus of power on which fascist systems are based. For he takes the world to be an affair of power concentrations requiring "the majority of men ... [to] be subservient to the machine," the instrument of their subordination being nothing more than fear. And thus, he says, "The Army functions best when you're frightened of the man above you, and contemptuous of your subordinates," since, when hate banks up in a man, he fights "a little better." All must be "fitted into a fear ladder" which so breaks their spirits as to make them tractable robots of the collectivity. "The natural role of twentieth-century man," he announces, "is anxiety"—the organization and management of which he, of course, intends that he himself shall play a large part in, since, for Cummings, it is precisely power that is the great erotic reality. And thus we are not surprised that the "Time Machine" discloses his marriage to have been a sexual disaster, or that it is in the lifeless abstractions of a chess game that he finds his principal recreation.

By reason of his rank, Cummings commands the decisive power on Anopopei; and he also commands a fierce and brutal articulateness. But in no other respect is he significantly different from the Boston Irishman Gallagher and the red-neck Wilson, from the little Chicago racketeer Polack and the Tulsa salesman Brown. For they, in their confused ineffectualness, represent merely an inchoate form of the same human reality which the General embodies. They all get what Red Valsen calls "the shitty end of the stick," but they would themselves be happy to wield that stick were it placed in their hands, for they are all "from the raucous stricken bosom of America." Red does himself have a compactness of identity that leads him to insist that he "won't take no crap from nobody," but his is an intelligence too primitive to enable him, finally, to withstand the inhuman forces arrayed against him. Indeed, the only figure equipped to enter the lists against Cummings is the young Harvard graduate, Lieutenant Hearn, who is able to take the General's measure as a "nerve end with no other desire than to find something to act upon." But for all of his commitment to the pieties of liberal democracy, he is, finally, very much like Mann's Hans Castorp, of whom he sometimes thinks, incapable of actualizing the dream of union between thought and action. Just as young Castorp, unable to align himself on either side of the duel between the humanist Settembrini and the Nietzschean Naphta, at last simply sinks into the "morally untidy universe" of the Magic Mountain, so it is in some measure with Hearn also. For though he, in his conversations with Cummings, can never bring himself to accept the cynical inhumanity of the General, he can never manage to summon any cogent defense of his Leftist sympathies and represents, presumably, in Mailer's pattern the unreliability of conventional liberalism, when faced by the totalitarian's hard, unyielding resoluteness. And Hearn's last state is no better than Castorp's: wanting to rid himself of the nuisance presented by his lieutenant, General Cummings puts him in charge of a platoon whose job it will be to climb the virtually insurmountable heights of Mt. Anaka by way of moving behind the Japanese lines for reconnaissance—and Hearn discovers that he enjoys the sensations of power attendant upon the leading of men: which is to say that he is entrained on a route leading down into the "morally untidy universe."

Before the patrol can be completed, however, Hearn is killed in an ambush, which he himself might have anticipated had not Sergeant Croft withheld from him information brought back from scouting of the terrain. In short, the humanist democrat is undone by the fascist bully (Cummings) and his vicious, unknowing subaltern (Croft). Thereafter, the reconnaissance is directed by the sergeant, and much of the finest writing in the book is devoted to an account of the platoon's anguished effort, under Croft's brutal discipline, to scale the mountain's defeating heights. And as these poor devils (Polack and Red and Gallagher and Martinez and Minetta), hour after hour and day after day, inch their way along this perilous stairway of rock and foliage—reeling and groaning, retching from exhaustion, and sometimes "weeping with the rapt taut sobs of fatigue"—their procession, always under the threat of

Croft's rifle, presents an extraordinary image of the help-
lessness of the human commonalty before the forces of
Ignorance and Anger and Cunning and Maleficence.

Finally, just as Croft begins to sense that the top is near,
he stumbles into a nest of hornets which, aroused, furious-
ly fling themselves upon the men, terrifying them to the
point of delirium. As, amidst their screams of pain, they
desperately flail at the violent wasps, the men hurl away
their rifles and, panic-stricken, begin to stumble down the
rocks. Then it is that Croft knows they are through, that
there is nothing for them to do but to return to headquar-
ters.

At the last, General Cummings' campaign to oust the
Japanese forces from the island, though victorious, in a
way collapses in irony—his victory, that is, being a matter
of accident, for, while he is away from the island seeking
naval support, the blundering Major Dalleson by sheer
chance prepares the maneuver that destroys the resistance.
So, just as nothing comes of the suffering enforced upon
Croft's platoon by his madness, so too nothing comes of
Cummings' elaborate calculations of strategy—a state of
affairs which, as it brings the novel to a close, makes a
marvelous figure of the absurdity of the Army and of
those larger human complexities for which it stands as an
emblem.

To speak of the novel in terms of its didactic intention
to produce a polemical rendering of the American reality—
of the easy malleability of its untutored multitudes (the
enlisted men), of the sinister ominousness of its professional reactionaries (General Cummings), of the bank-
ruptcy of its liberalism (Hearn)—is, of course, to over-
schematize the density of the material which Mailer drama-
tizes, as it is also in some measure to falsify the "feel" of
his story. For the young man who produced this book was
a natural fabulist whose mind was unviolated by any

compunctions against story; and, with his genius for inventing incident and describing the land he had himself encountered as an American soldier in Leyte and Luzon, he created a great sprawling novel so brilliantly vibrant with felt life that its most immediate effect is not likely to be that of didacticism. *The Naked and the Dead* is, nevertheless, a book deeply rooted in a body of doctrine which, however unsystematized, gathers a certain coherence from its determination to elicit an abjuratory response to the brutality and cynicism that Mailer's army experience had led him to regard as behind the great central drift of American society. And the prophetic role which his parable appears to attribute to General Cummings and Sergeant Croft, as well as to Lieutenant Hearn, makes it clear that he conceived this drift to be one which might well be propelling us forward into a new world in which the elementary decencies of justice and honor and plain dealing would be held at such a discount as to render us vulnerable to precisely the kind of cancerous fascism that our huge military effort of the forties had been intended to cauterize. It is, in short, at this level of its implication that his novel of 1948 may be seen to be not so much about the events of the Second World War as about a certain "psychic havoc" that lay behind the American involvement in that great conflict.

*        *        *

Mailer's second novel, *Barbary Shore*, which appeared in 1951, continues the assessment of the American condition begun in his first work, though its manner is strikingly different. It is a caustic, mordant, garrulous book, the product of a period in his life of great personal stress which he has recounted in his *Advertisements for Myself*, where he speaks of how the huge success of his first novel suddenly "blasted" him into a profound perplexity about what his future course should be. He had overnight entered the world of celebrity, only to find it a most perilous place indeed, where the people one met in New York all seemed to be "wired with shocks for the small electrocution of oneself." So, as he says, "I traveled scared, excited, and nervous, ridden by the question which everyone else was ready to ask and which I was forever asking of myself: had this first published novel been all of my talent? Or would my next book be better?" But perhaps the more deeply nagging question concerned whether the next book in its character ought to be something very much different from *The Naked and the Dead.* This was the really focal issue of his inner colloquy: " . . . was I to write about Brooklyn streets, or my mother and father, or another war novel . . . [or] was I to do the book of the returning veteran . . . ?" Was he, in short, to go on producing the kind of novel that Dos Passos and Farrell had taught him how to control? But, as he came gradually to feel, to all these options "success had been a lobotomy," and this inordinately ambitious young man concluded, therefore, that he had no choice now but "to accept the private heat and fatigue of setting out by . . . [himself] to cut a track through a new wild." His decision was "to step into the war of the enormous present"—that new war being called the Cold War—and to try as a novelist to capture "the air of our time, authority and nihilism stalking one another in the orgiastic hollow of this century." And the result was the book of 1951.

In his thoughtful essay on Mailer, Richard Foster places *Barbary Shore* in that category of fiction German criticism speaks of as *Bildungsroman.* And it would seem, indeed, to be a novel of development, for "its narrative substance is the hero's education for life in our time—or re-education, since he is suffering from amnesia somewhat inexplicitly induced by war and the breakdown of traditional political idealism."[4] Like Saul Bellow's *Dangling Man* (which—in its sombre, claustral atmosphere—it somewhat resembles) the novel sets its main action in a rooming house. Here, in Brooklyn Heights, the young amnesiac Michael Lovett settles, after amassing a nest egg of five hundred dollars which he hopes to stretch out over the half year to be devoted to the writing of his projected novel. He is the first-person narrator of Mailer's tale, the omniscient standpoint of the effaced annalist in the first book being now abandoned. And "Mikey" Lovett's testimony concerns his tangled encounters with the other tenants in the seedy hostel presided over by the blowzy ex-burlesque queen who calls herself Guinevere.

Very shortly after he takes up residence in Guinevere's establishment, Lovett finds himself drawn into a congenial relationship with another tenant, the laconic and embittered *isolé* McLeod. Turning himself out in "the anonymous clothing of a man who buys his garments as cheaply as possible," McLeod works as a department store window dresser. But the impression McLeod conveys of a timid person who "would sell the birthright he had never enjoyed for regular work and security" is most ironically disproportionate to what has been the actuality of his life. For, as we eventually discover, he is a man of acute intelligence who was formerly an operative first of the Communist underground and then, after the consummation of the Nazi-Soviet pact, of the American State Depart-

---

[4]Richard Foster, *Norman Mailer*, Pamphlets on American Writers, no. 73 (Minneapolis: University of Minnesota Press, 1968), p. 13.

ment until his Leftist allegiances finally required him to break with what he felt to be the increasingly reactionary alignments of federal Washington.

Nor is another of Guinevere's lodgers, Leroy Hollingsworth, quite the man he at first seems to be. He invites Lovett into his room one evening for a can of beer—a room strewn with soiled laundry and empty beer cans and overflowing wastebaskets, the "desk littered with pencil shavings, inkstains, cigarette butts, and a broken box of letter paper." But Hollingsworth appears strangely unrelated to his room. "His cloth summer pants were clean, his open shirt was fresh, his hair was combed, he was shaved." And Lovett takes this freckled young man with his corn-colored cowlick and bright blue eyes, his trim build and easy grace of movement and polite talk about the weather, to be a "simple small-town boy come to the big city" and, as he looks about the room, can see "the places in which he had slept through his boyhood: a bed, a Bible, and in the corner a baseball bat perhaps." Yes, Lovett thinks, "He was obviously from a small town. . . ." And no doubt this innocent-looking stranger whose features are "without distinction" does come from somewhere in the heartland of America. Indeed, given the representative role he seems finally to be assigned in the novel's allegory, it is important for Lovett's surmise about his origins to be correct. But however authentic an exemplar Hollingsworth may be of "middle America," the innocence Lovett initially presumes is, again, utterly disproportionate to the actuality. For Hollingsworth is in fact an FBI agent operating under an alias. It appears that, following McLeod's departure from the State Department, the authorities there discovered a "little object" of great value to be missing; and, since the presumption is that it was stolen by McLeod, Hollingsworth has been delegated to recover it—which is why he has engaged one of Guinevere's rooms.

Hollingsworth proves to be a cunning and relentless detective, but, beneath his scrubbed and tidy exterior, this representative of grass-roots America turns out to be an unpleasant human being—whose only politics amount to nativist phobias about Communism, whose only ethic appears to be one of self-advantage, a man who leeringly boasts of his "interesting experiences with the lady downstairs" (Guinevere), who makes lewd proposals to waitresses in restaurants, and who likes pornographic novels but wonders if they should be "allowed," since many are written by "Bolshevists" and contain "atheistic things." And the ambiguousness of his pious professions of distaste for "atheistic things" is nicely suggested by the fact that the only icon of his Christian faith to be found in his room is a little piece of gimcrackery, a "phosphorescent cross printed on cardboard" which makes a lurid glow in the dark. Here, indeed, is an unsavory instance of the kind of homunculus produced by a "mass society," a creature without even the merest shred of humanizing culture and wholly at the mercy of his fears and appetites—one not even equipped to be a reliable tool of the Leviathan, as is made evident finally by his decision to appropriate the "little object" to himself once he lays hands upon it. His superiors have concealed its exact nature, but he has pieced together enough information to conjecture that its value must be immense. So he intends to abscond with it, and thus he is careful to withhold from Washington any accurate intelligence about the progress of his investigations.

It is appropriate that Hollingsworth's partner in this scheme should be his landlady Guinevere, "the lady downstairs" with whom he has "interesting experiences." For she, in her mindless greed and vulgarity, is also ordained by the novel to be an exemplar of that demotic atavism in the lower depths of American life which presents an earnest of the kind of barbarity that may be bred in democratic soil. She is in fact McLeod's wife, and, as such (in Diana Trilling's shrewd notation), illustrates the instability of the human material with which "the revolutionary idealist has perforce had to align himself. . . ."[5] They dwell under the same roof but no longer occupy common quarters or maintain any semblance of keeping their marriage intact. Indeed, Guinevere makes her bedroom available to first one and then another of her lodgers and seems always to have been prepared to peddle her flamboyant sexuality, for she freely relates to Lovett "story after story about this man and that lover, about presents she had accepted and presents spurned. . . . 'I been every kind of woman you'd want, Lovett.' " So fascinated is she with her sordid past as courtesan and burlesque queen that she supposes a fictional version of her career would be "worth a million bucks" to a Hollywood film studio, and she urges Lovett to prepare the script. She is a sharp, unprincipled, predatory slut who, once her liaison with Hollingsworth is established and she discovers the nature of his mission, is quick to propose that they get hold for themselves of the "thingamajig" which McLeod has and sell it to some foreign power. "They'd make us royalty," she says. And when Hollingsworth presses her to be more specific about just where they might go, she says, "Anywhere. To the ends of the earth. To Barbary. . . ." But, of course, this is a journey that needs not to be undertaken, since, given their essential depravity, this is just where they already are—on the shore of Barbary.

[5]Diana Trilling, "The Radical Moralism of Norman Mailer," in *The Creative Present: Notes on Contemporary American Fiction*, ed. Nona Balakian and Charles Simmons (Garden City, N.Y.: Doubleday & Co., 1963), p. 156.

There is one other resident in Guinevere's rooming house who plays an important role in the action of the novel, a girl named Lannie Madison, who, like McLeod, has been a devotee of radical politics and who has been plunged into "fathomless desperation" by the failures of the Marxist movement. She is a girl quite unhinged by Trotsky's assassination and by the amoralism of Communist *Realpolitik* signalized by that event. "Save me," her monomania prompts her to cry, even in her moment of sexual transport with Lovett. And, in this young hysteriac's demonology, McLeod figures now as the chief image of that great treachery which brought an end to the last and the best hope of the twentieth century. "Your people," she shouts at him in reference to Trotsky's murder—"your people raised the ax, and the last blood of revolutionary mankind, his poor blood, ran into the carpet." She speaks, of course, more truly than she knows, for McLeod, as he later concedes, did indeed play a minor part in the drama—not large enough to have blood on his hands but managing an "infinitesimal part of the operation" and smelling "a little of what was to come," taking care of a detail here and there and being simply an efficient cog in the vast machine of conspiracy. So Lannie, filled with chagrin now at her earlier innocence in supposing "that there was a world we could make," finds in the renegade Communist McLeod a symbol of everything by which her great dream has been undone—which is what permits her at last to support Hollingsworth in his brutal inquisitions of one whom she regards as an "undertaker of the revolution," her readiness as a disenchanted idealist to join with the forces of reaction finding its analogue, in the stresses of physical relationship, in her lesbian affair with Guinevere.

But nothing ever comes of Hollingsworth's inquisitions. Again and again he interrogates McLeod, who does at last agree to surrender the "little object"—though, even at this late stage in the novel, what precisely it is remains a mystery, so that we are left to surmise that it is nothing so simple, say, as a piece of microfilm carrying some secret formula of military technology but something more, some great Revelation perhaps of how the powers of Darkness may be quelled and the human future guaranteed. His promise to surrender this talisman, however, is intended only to be momentarily off-putting, and, just before he is murdered by Hollingsworth (in Guinevere's suite), he hands it over in an envelope to Lovett—with these words: "As Lenin said to the priest Gapon, 'Study, little father, or you will lose your head.' You hear, Lovett?" Lovett nods. And, at the end, we are told that McLeod's will contained but one bequest: "To Michael Lovett to whom, at the end of my life and for the first time within it, I find myself capable of the rudiments of selfless friendship, I bequeath in heritage the remnants of my socialist culture. . . . And may he be alive to see the rising of the Phoenix."

"So," says Lovett, "the heritage passed on to me . . . and I went out into the world. If I fled down the alley which led from that rooming house, it was only to enter another, and then another. . . . Meanwhile, vast armies mount themselves, the world revolves, the traveller clutches his breast. . . . The storm approaches its thunderhead, and it is apparent that the boat drifts ever closer to shore"—to the shore, that is, of Barbary.

It is a very bleak conclusion, indeed. For what is being said is that the revolutionary idealism that emanated from the Russian Revolution (McLeod) is exhausted; that *les foules* (Guinevere) with whom that idealism wanted to make common cause are in fact often prepared to enter into partnership with just those forces of reaction (Hollingsworth) that would destroy it; that, indeed, the Popular Front mentality (Lannie Madison) of the time before

World War II is become so deranged as to be capable of electing a similar partnership; and that the only alternative to the incipient fascism (Hollingsworth) lying just beneath the surface of American life rests with a confused and incompetent liberalism (the amnesiac Lovett) which is forever clutching "the remnants of . . . socialist culture" to its breast, as it flees down first one alley and then another. So it is, as the novel says in its final sentence, that "the blind . . . lead the blind, and the deaf shout warnings to one another until their voices are lost"—as we drift ever closer to Barbary Shore. We are, in short, at "the end of ideology," at last bereft of any large possibility of settling the American future by political means—the proof of this extremity which the novel offers being the fact that the key to our redemption lies in some indefinable "little object."

Now the despair of politics expressed by *Barbary Shore* proved nettling in the early 1950s, and the novel was almost universally declared to be a leaden disaster. In a brilliant sentence Norman Podhoretz has spoken of it as "a book such as might have been written by one of those brooding, distracted students who haunt the pages of Russian literature."[6] But something more bracing was wanted in those years: so this dark, sour, threatening book—with its air of "authority and nihilism stalking one another in the orgiastic hollow of this century"—was biliously rejected. Mailer has candidly recounted in *Advertisements for Myself* how nearly the resulting disappointment and self-doubt brought him to utter psychological collapse. But he is right in his suggestion (in his *Advertisements*) that the fundamental intuitions expressed in *Barbary Shore* presaged a basic line of his future development. For—after his

[6]Norman Podhoretz, "Norman Mailer: The Embattled Vision," in *Doings and Undoings: The Fifties and After in American Writing* (New York: Farrar, Straus & Co., 1964), p. 196.

vigorous support of Henry Wallace's presidential candidacy
on the Progressive Party ticket of 1948 and his immediately subsequent agonizing over the limited range of options
in public life facing the American people—not since (withal
his spirited performance as a candidate in the New York
mayoralty race of 1969 and his involvement in the anti-
Vietnam peace movements of the late sixties) has he conceived the customary realm of empirical politics to be the
arena of our salvation. And, after the book of 1951, this
foreswearing of conventional civic enterprise was further
instanced by the novel which followed it four years later.

*    *    *

The epigraph of *The Deer Park* (1955) presents a quota-
tion from a French account of that Deer Park which Louis
XV kept at Versailles, "that gorge of innocence and virtue
in which were engulfed so many victims"—girls collected
from "all the corners of the kingdom" by the sovereign's
"band of pimps and madames" and who, after they had
been polished and dressed and perfumed and furnished
"with all the means of seduction that art could provide,"
were then presented to "the jaded passions of the sultan."
And the novel wants, of course, to suggest that this infer-
nal playground of Louis XV may be taken as a metaphor
of the Deer Park, or jungle, which America itself has
become, now that its moralities and patterns of life are
rooted in a malaise—of agues and calentures—not unlike
that which long ago prevailed at Versailles.

The particular region of America which Mailer here
chooses as his microcosm is a resort for the Hollywood
film colony in the cactus wilds of southern California, a
town called Desert D'Or, which appears to be a facsimile
of Palm Springs. It is a place built since the Second World
War, where "everything is in the present tense" and where

(like the Hollywood of Nathanael West's *The Day of the Locust*) everything is other than what it appears to be. The stores, for example, look "like anything but stores":

> In those places which sold clothing, no clothing was laid out, and you waited in a modern living room while salesmen opened panels in the wall to exhibit summer suits. . . . There was a jewelry store built like a cabin cruiser; from the street one peeped through a porthole to see a thirty-thousand-dollar necklace hung on the silver antlers of a piece of driftwood.

And the hotels—the Yacht Club and the Debonair and the Desert D'Or Arms—are not hotels but arrangements (hidden behind elaborately sculpted shrubberies) of carports and swimming pools shaped like free-form coffee tables and pastel bungalows, all lit up at night by Japanese lanterns strung to the tropical trees. Everything is parched by the searing sun, so that all human activity takes place within the air-conditioned bars and cocktail lounges and night clubs which are "made to look like a jungle, an underwater grotto, or the lounge of a modern movie theater," in which one never knows whether it is night or day.

It is to this place, wearing his flying wings and first lieutenant's uniform, that a young veteran of the Korean War comes—Sergius O'Shaugnessy by name (the narrator of the novel)—with fourteen thousand dollars won at poker in a Tokyo hotel room just before he was flown home. Though "still intact," he is so just barely, for, like Michael Lovett, he is one who has been maimed in "the orgiastic hollow of this century," not by amnesia but by sexual impotence. This disability is the result of a psychological collapse suffered during the War, after the realization broke in upon him of the enormities in which he was implicated by having been involved in the raining of napalm on thousands of helpless Korean peasants. So, having

now been mustered out of the Air Force, with nowhere to
go and "no family to visit" (for he was orphaned in early
childhood), he drifts into Desert D'Or, diminished and
spent, to view the scene and, as it may be, to regather his
bearings. And it is his consciousness that forms a reflector
of the strange underworld presented by the glittering artifice of this God-forsaken town.

Of the various residents of the resort Sergius shortly
meets, it is to the film director Charles Francis Eitel that
he finds himself most drawn. Eitel is an artist-technician of
considerable talent who has been blacklisted by the movie
industry for refusing to give information on his former
Leftist associates to a Congressional investigating committee. Now, exiled from the film capital and with his finan-
cial reserves steadily dwindling, he is living in Desert D'Or,
where he is desperately attempting to recover the command of his craft he once possessed before he began his
long journey down the road of compromise with the gross
commercialism of the moguls running his studio, Supreme
Pictures. Despite the fine originality expressed in the force
and inventiveness of his early work, over so long a period
did he specialize in producing the phony confections readily saleable to an undemanding public that he has lost an
essential integrity of feeling and imagination: so the film
he is now trying to design remains, in its fancied greatness,
only a dream which he is unable to substantialize in a
workable script.

Indeed, the burden of Eitel's defeat and his growing fear
might well be unbearable, were it not for the girl who
becomes his mistress at Desert D'Or, Elena Esposito—a
young woman whom Mailer strangely presents in the terms
of Tennessee Williams, as one who has been badly used by
many men and who by her own maltreatment has been
made gentle and compassionate and "kind." She is without
any gifts of intellect or refinements of culture, but her

warm sensuality and the generous affirmativeness which she offers have the effect of restoring to Eitel a capacity for hope and confidence that had very nearly been destroyed by the failures of recent years. So enheartening for him is their relationship that at last he begins once more, in working on his script, to find a kind of access to the creativity that has long been lost, and the resultant blossoming of assurance brings him a new gift for fronting the men of power in "the capital" (as Hollywood is always spoken of) who had heartlessly thrust him out once they thought his day was over, men such as old Herman Teppis, the head of Supreme Pictures, and his son-in-law, the producer Collie Munshin. And they in turn, facing a man who no longer exudes the air of defeat, begin once more to bestow the industry's smile of approval and to hold forth the promise of reinstatement—if he will only consent to be a cooperative witness before the Congressional committee. So, having tasted the gall of exclusion and doubting his capacity much longer to endure utter abandonment, he does finally submit to their yoke, knowing all the while that his surrender to the world of Herman Teppis proves him (as he says in a colloquy that he imagines between Sergius and himself) to "have lost the final desire of the artist, the desire which tells us that when all else is lost, when love is lost and adventure, pride of self, and pity, there still remains that world we may create, more real to us, more real to others than the mummery of what happens, passes, and is gone."

The *dramatic* proof which the novel offers of Eitel's last state being even worse than the first is the fact of his having begun at the end (though now married to Elena) an affair with his ex-wife and Supreme Pictures' great siren, the star Lulu Meyers. She is vacationing in Desert D'Or at the time of Sergius's arrival, and, though it is with her that he recovers his sexual potency, she is not to be thought of as exemplifying any redemptive principle. For she is the quintessential embodiment in the novel of the spangled speciousness distinguishing the society which is here being analyzed, this dimpled blonde with her throaty voice and little turned-up nose who is, in every aspect of her personality, a creature of the mass media. "On the few times I would be allowed to spend the night with her," says Sergius, "I would wake up to see Lulu writing an idea for publicity in the notebook she kept on her bed table. . . ." And, as he tells us, when they were together in a restaurant,

> It always seemed to her as if the conversation at another table was more interesting than what she heard at her own. She had the worry that she was missing a word of gossip, a tip, a role in a picture, a financial transaction, a . . . it did not matter; something was happening somewhere else, something of importance, something she could not afford to miss. Therefore, eating with her was like sleeping with her; if one was cut by the telephone, the other was rubbed by her itch to visit from table to table. . . .

She is convinced that her breasts will droop as she grows older, and so she insists that Sergius be careful when he touches them. She is a consummate narcissist, her entire existence a ceremony performed before mirrors; and this little celluloid doll—who, when stampeded by autograph-hounds, gurgles about what a "wonderful life" she has—is, therefore, a caricature of a woman. So we find nothing incongruous in Herman Teppis wanting, for the sake of the publicity and Lulu's Bimmler rating, to marry her off to the homosexual leading man Teddy Pope.

Now the sinister and diabolical intendant of call-girls in Desert D'Or, Marion Faye, regards all these people—the hortative old lecher and ruthless tycoon, "Uncle" Herman

Teppis; his clever, grasping huckster of a son-in-law, Collie Munshin; the matinee goddess Lulu Meyers; even, one suspects, his own mother, the sleekly handsome ex-nightclub singer, Dorothea O'Faye (who presides over a big house which is called The Hangover and who boasts that she's been everywhere and done everything)—he regards the town's whole gang as "slobs." And Faye is in many respects—far more so than Sergius, who forever remains a somewhat shadowy and problematic presence—the moral center of the book. For it is this young pimp who sees, with a burning clarity, the essential decadence not just of Desert D'Or and "the capital" in the background but, more significantly, of the larger American reality of which he considers the Hollywood scene to be the most revealing symbol. He is a saint turned upside down whose stratagem for heroism in a rotten world is one which Baudelaire designated as *dandysme*—which is to say that he defends himself against rampant depravity and achieves his own personal splendor by converting himself into a creature of artifice. He chooses to assert his freedom by refusing all ties, all obligations, all commandments. He speaks only in order to baffle. He establishes his independence of natural desires by cultivating the arts of sadism and debauchery, as he nullifies his loneliness by cultivating the art of offering offense. Cruelty in all its forms is repugnant to him, but, since his dandyism requires him to consider "no pleasure [to be] greater than that obtained from a conquered repugnance," he fights all compassionate impulses "with the fury of a man looking for purity" and is frightfully cruel to the vulnerable and the helpless. "You know," says Sergius to Faye in one of their conversations, "you're just a religious man turned inside out." But, though Faye seems to be a little irritated by the remark and says in response, "You have a brain like a scrambled egg," O'Shaugnessy comes very close to the fundamental truth about this Luciferian *élégant*. For Faye is one committed, with something like a monastic rigor, to the disciplines of the *via negativa*. He is convinced that, when all is tarnished and corrupt, the only way into authenticity is that which Conrad long ago foresaw—namely, immersion in "the destructive element." Which is perhaps why he never sleeps behind a locked door, in order that the furies of the night in Desert D'Or may never be shut out. That is to say, his decision has been that, in a debased and villainous society, one must undertake to play the role of villain, descending to the very heart of darkness; and, in this way perhaps, one may "push to the end . . . and come out—he did not know where, but there was experience beyond experience, there was something. Of that, he was certain." So his confidence that the world he knows is destined for annihilation does not at all cause him to despair: his mind is filled with apocalyptic visions of a great final cataclysm—but "Let it come. . . . Let it come, Faye begged, like a man praying for rain, let it come and clear the rot and the stench and the stink, let it come for all of everywhere, just so it comes and the world stands clear in the white dead dawn."

It is, indeed, behind such a mystical illuminism of the Negative Way that the novel appears to line itself up. It does, to be sure, admit into its purview those rough actualities of concrete politics that were signalizing for Mailer at the time a great drift in American life toward a basically totalitarian society. Just as the country's incipient fascism was represented in *The Naked and the Dead* by General Cummings and in *Barbary Shore* by Hollingsworth, so, too, *The Deer Park* is shadowed by the Congressional committee whose concern to extirpate subversive dissent is intended to be remindful of that whole ugly McCarthy era in the 1950s—and the bruising encounter between O'Shaugnessy and the Special Investigators who come at the committee's behest in search of information on Eitel provides one important occasion in the novel for its direct contemplation of the fascist menace. But, as Mailer had said in the spring of 1952 in his contribution to the *Partisan Review's* symposium on "Our Country and Our Culture," "Today, the enemy is vague...." And thus the abdication from reformist politics first hinted at in *Barbary Shore* is even more fully expressed in the book of 1955 where, most especially through the focal figure of Marion Faye, Mailer's purpose would seem to be that of saying that renewal of life awaits not some new scheme of political reconstruction but a sort of death, a sort of descent—into "the destructive element." What is required, as the novel suggests in its final sentence, is "the connection of new circuits," for only by managing this feat do we stand any chance of getting out of the Deer Park.

*       *       *

The degree to which his development over the past fifteen years has clarified our sense of Mailer's basic orientation enables us now to see that there was, indeed, a very direct line of thought leading from the concern for "new circuits" to one of the most crucial statements of his career, the famous essay on "The White Negro" which Irving Howe published in *Dissent* in 1957 and which, as moral scripture, has had an influence on the radical young of our period so deep as to be well-nigh incalculable. Here, amidst his elaborate exposition of the metaphysics of "philosophical psychopathy," we can now see his portrait of Marion Faye to have been his first venture in setting forth the idea of Hipsterism; and the essay of 1957—in its concept of the "psychic outlaw"—can today be recognized as Mailer's first systematic effort at defining a pattern of life alternative to that which (in the language he was regularly thereafter to employ) leads to "cancer."

The Hipster—who is the man fully alert to the absolute precariousness of the human enterprise in our time—is the analogue in Mailer's universe of Baudelaire's Dandy. He is "the man who knows that if our collective condition is to live with [the ever present possibilities of] instant death by atomic war ... or with a slow death by conformity with every creative and rebellious instinct stifled ... why then the only life-giving answer is to accept the terms of death, to live with death as immediate danger, to divorce oneself from society, to exist without roots, to set out on that uncharted journey into the rebellious imperatives of the self." In a bad world, in a totalitarian (or partially totalitarian) world, where all the pressures of a techno-cratic society are calculated to obliterate any sense of the sanctity of the private self, the Hipster is the man who has the courage to step outside the conventional orders of life and give his fealty to the "incandescent consciousness" that he carries within himself of the myriad possibilities of human fulfillment contained within his own selfhood. And thus to the herd mentality of a mass culture he will appear to be a psychopath. But, in Mailer's lexicon, to "be able to feel oneself ... [to] know one's desires, one's rages, one's anguish," is to be a "philosophical psychopath"—or, as he likes to say, it is to be an "existentialist." It is the reso-nance of implication belonging to the former term, how-ever, which is more in keeping with the basic stress of the manifesto of 1957, for, there, the heaviest emphasis falls on the essentially antinomian posture of Hip.[7] Since he

7In his varying use of the terms Hipsterism and Hip, Mailer's nomen-clature presents some ambiguity, for the terms often appear to be interchangeable—yet, on certain occasions, they are so used as to imply some delicate shade of difference. But, since this nuance appears at best to be something highly fugitive, it is unlikely that any great violence will be done to his meaning by our simply treating the two terms homonymously.

conceives the power of his orgasm to be the great clue to how well he is living and since orgasm is his therapy, the Hipster's operative norms are furnished not by tribal dogma and tradition but by instinct: he "knows instinctively that to express a forbidden impulse actively is far more beneficial to him than merely to confess the desire in the safety of a doctor's room." Indeed, he may even permit himself murder "out of the necessity to purge his violence, for if he cannot empty his hatred than he cannot love." He is one living too close to the secrets of his own inwardness to allow himself to be in any way trapped by social restraints and circumscriptions. Thus, being equipped against all the attritions of conformity by his monkish dedication to the mystery of his own life, he is a man—in some ways like Marion Faye—who is "crazy," who is "with it," who is "cool," who does only what his "need" prompts him to do. His sole commitment is to "the rebellious imperatives of the self."

Now Mailer calls this new urban adventurer who drifts out into the streets at night "looking for action" a "white Negro," because he imagines the Negro—for whom survival has perforce always been a matter of living with danger—to be the source of Hip. "Knowing in the cells of his existence that life was war, nothing but war, the Negro," he says,

> (all exceptions admitted) could rarely afford the sophisticated inhibitions of civilization, and so he kept for his survival the art of the primitive, he lived in the enormous present, he subsisted for his Saturday night kicks, relinquishing the pleasures of the mind for the more obligatory pleasures of the body, and in his music he gave voice to the character and quality of his existence, to his rage and the infinite variations of joy, lust, languor, growl, cramp, pinch, scream and despair of his orgasm.

His image of the Negro here is no doubt being presented as a metaphor; but its affrontiveness is, nevertheless, hardly to be gainsaid—as James Baldwin was in due time to remind him, in an essay[8] in which he remarked what is obviously the case, that Mailer's lewdly scurrilous comic strip is only one more maligning advertisement of the old *mystique* about the Negro as sexual orgiast which has been a cause of so much tragic mischief in the course of American history. But there is no recorded expression of Mailer's ever having felt any embarrassment about this indiscretion, and one may well doubt that he has, for there is more than a little evidence in his writing of a strange captivity to attitudes of condescension where the Negro is concerned—as, for example, in the virtuoso piece in *The Presidential Papers* devoted to his account of the proceedings that surrounded the first encounter in the ring between the prizefighters Floyd Patterson and Sonny Liston in 1962, where Mailer, as he recalls his own meeting with the "Supreme Spade" (Sonny Liston), manages, for all of what was actually Liston's massive stolidity, to fancy that he picked up a "hint of corny old darky laughter, cottonfield giggles. . . ."

His treacherous ambivalences of feeling about the Negro, however, belong only to the periphery of his essay of 1957, since its central intention is not that of advancing a racial thesis but is, rather, that of setting forth a new possibility for surviving the twentieth century—namely, that which is incarnate in the "psychic outlaw." By 1957 his brooding on the American condition had brought Mailer to the conclusion that ours is a time in which the Enemy is "vague," because the Enemy has become nothing else than a deathlike depletion of the nation's moral substance, has become that epidemic madness induced by

[8]See James Baldwin, "The Black Boy Looks at the White Boy," in *Nobody Knows My Name* (New York: Dial Press, 1961).

plastics and sleeping pills and frozen foods and sexual repression and the search for the kind of security promised by the FBI. And he had decided that, in a time when we suffer a plague in the soul and "some unendurable stricture of eternity," it will be fruitless to look for any way out of our distress in politics. For politics is an affair of calculations and statistics, an affair merely of a kind of arithmetic which at best will yield nothing more than a new "package with new consumer interest"—"the old apple pie still tasting of soggy cardboard and cheap flour, but the container is new—it has a picture on its cellophane cover which motivation research has discovered is more effective than the old cover for selling apple pie" (Preface to *The Presidential Papers*).

No, Mailer was convinced, it is not some new scheme of politics that we need: on the contrary, what is required is a new path for the imagination, nothing less indeed than a new humanism, and it was of this new "existential grasp of the nature of reality" that he presented his Hipster as a kind of prophetic symbol. For it is he, the psychic outlaw, the "existential hero," who reveals how we may "open the limits of the possible"—not by fleeing from the abyss but by confronting it, not by making any pact with the attenuated, mechanized, hygienic world of modern technocracy but by boldly entering into "the mysteries of murder, suicide, incest, orgy, orgasm and Time."

Since Mailer's metaphors—of psychopathy and orgy and violence and death—were shockingly nihilistic and since he did himself sometimes seem to forget that they were metaphors, "The White Negro" was considered by many of its readers to be an exercise in obscurantism by a bombed-out writer who had, indeed, fallen into the sloughs of nihilism. But, as we now look back upon this vehement manifesto, from the perspective afforded by Mailer's subsequent career, it ought surely to be clear that, far from having any nihilistic impulse as its basic motive, it was most essentially informed by a great rage over the stifling mediocrity of the human landscape in mid-century America and by a great desire to redeem, however radically, a world that had become unlovable. The universe it was evoking was, in short, very much a universe of good and evil.

Indeed, it was the moralizing passion that had at last been completely unthrottled in the essay of 1957 which seems now to be the major shaping force in the series of brilliant miscellanies that Mailer began at intervals shortly thereafter to issue—first, *Advertisements for Myself* in 1959, then *The Presidential Papers* in 1963, and *Cannibals and Christians* in 1966. In these extraordinary collections of journalism and personal confession and sermonizing, the voice we think of today as distinctly Mailer's takes on its characteristic pitch and tone—dogmatic and pugnacious and always exigent, yet irrepressibly gay and playful, never pompous but never fearful of eloquence (whether in the lyric or the declarative mode), and, finally, for all of its frequently outrageous indiscretions, somehow endearing in a way quite unparalleled by the impress upon us of that of any of the other writers of the first rank on the current American scene. The presence emerging from these books is not so much that of a novelist doing part-time duty in the genres of social and political criticism as it is that of the public man who (as he frankly concedes in the *Advertisements*) "will settle for nothing less than making a revolution in the consciousness of our time." He is the occupant of a pulpit who wants to elicit a sort of *metanoia* in the souls of his constituency. For since God's own destiny must surely in part be contingent on our keeping faith with that covenant in which we with Him are primordially bound, when we by our heedlessness and perversity break the covenant, then—as he warns in the *Adver-*

*tisements*—God Himself may be "in danger of dying." So this "smiling public man," passionate and not afraid to be foolish, wants (as Richard Foster has so well said) "to steal back, for the languishing forces of 'God,' some of the energies of life which have passed over to the forces of darkness."[9] And it is for this purpose that he seeks to

> lie down where all the ladders start
> In the foul rag-and-bone shop of the heart.

What is astonishing in the performance represented by these books is the prodigious capacity it reflects for paying the strictest attention to the entire stretch of American life (its politics, its sports, its architecture, its literature, its popular arts, its racial collisions, its sexual styles). And equally dazzling is the singular brilliance with which this panorama, in all its particularity and multifariousness, is described and figured forth in the full density of this "enormous present." It is a hot, vernacular, cranky, sceptical, rapid, circling prose that will doubtless in later years be felt more fully to have captured the hum and buzz of the fifties and sixties than any other body of testimony belonging to the period. His report (in *Cannibals and Christians*) on the Goldwater convention of 1964 in San Francisco makes a representative instance of the style. In recalling, for example, one of the press conferences at the Hilton Hotel held by Governor Scranton of Pennsylvania, who was, of course, at the time seeking the Republican presidential nomination, he tells us how Scranton

> stood there like a saint, a most curious kind of saint. If he had been an actor he would have played the Dauphin to Ingrid Bergman's Joan of Arc. He was obviously, on superficial study, a weak and stubborn man. One felt he

[9]Foster, *Norman Mailer*, p. 27.

had been spoiled when he was young by a lack of testing. It was not that he lacked bravery, it was that he had lacked all opportunity to be brave for much too long, and now he was not so much engaged in a serious political struggle as in a puberty rite. It was incredible that this pleasant urbane man, so self-satisfied, so civilized, so reasonable, so innocent of butchers' tubs and spleens and guts (that knowledge which radiates with full ceremony off Khrushchev's halo), should be now in fact the man the Eastern Establishment had picked as their candidate for President. He had a fatal flaw to his style, he was just very slightly delicate the way, let us say, a young Madison Avenue executive will seem petulant next to the surly vigor of a president of a steel corporation. Scranton had none of the heft of a political jockstrapper like Goldwater; no, rather he had the big wide thin-lipped mouth of a clown—hopeless!

Or, again, in the same piece he tells us how, at a caucus of the Florida delegation one hot afternoon "in a dingy little downstairs banquet room" at the Beverly Plaza,

Barry sat in the front, a spotlight on him, a silver film of perspiration adding to his patina, and the glasses, those black-framed glasses, took on that odd life of their own, that pinched severity, that uncompromising idealism which made Goldwater kin to the tight-mouthed and the lonely. Talking in a soft modest voice, he radiated at this moment the skinny boyish sincerity of a fellow who wears glasses but is determined nonetheless to have a good time. Against all odds. It was not unreminiscent of Arthur Miller: that same mixture of vast solemnity and unspoiled boyhood, a sort of shucks and aw shit in the voice.

And, as for Goldwater's supporters, the worst of the professionals

looked like divinity students who had been expelled
from the seminary for embezzling class funds and still
felt they were nearest to J.C.—there was a dark blank
fanaticism in their eyes. And the best of the Goldwater
professionals were formidable, big rangy men, some
lean, some flabby, with the hard distasteful look of
topflight investigators for fire-insurance companies. . . .

The rank and file of the Goldwaterites, however, as one
met them in hotel lobbies, were people who "had an
insane sting to their ideas—they were for birching America's bare bottom where Come-you-nisms collected: white
and Negro equality; sexual excess; Jew ideas; dirty linen,
muddled thinking, lack of respect for the Constitution":

> Not for nothing did the White Anglo-Saxon Protestant
> have a five-year subscription to *Reader's Digest* and
> *National Geographic*, high colonics and arthritis, silver-
> rimmed spectacles, punched-out bellies, and that air of
> controlled schizophrenia which is the merit badge for
> having spent one's life on Main Street.

So it is that this voice—remarkable at once in the splendid virtuosity of its witty rhetoric and in the marvelling
surprise at American humanity that it registers—so it is
that it records in the *Advertisements* and *The Presidential
Papers* and *Cannibals and Christians* the response elicited
from a crotchety, ebullient, wonderfully intelligent human
being by the troubled land presided over by John Kennedy
and Lyndon Johnson. It is a voice always urgent and filled
with apocalyptic intensities, for history is felt to have
become a kind of nightmare, the Goths are at the gates, a
"shit storm" is coming. And always, therefore, the voice
being heard in these books wants to hold forth to a
plague-ridden people the possibility of a "new consciousness," the chance of a new life, of life in the "existential"
mode. So (to use a term for which Mailer has a certain

fondness) the "armature" of these books is his concept of "existential politics"—which is not a politics of calculations and statistics (yielding up only the old apple pie in a new package) but a politics whose basic premise is the asserted possibility of a certain kind of heroism wherewith the individual and the nation (buried now under "Rightist encomiums for the FBI, programmatic welfare from the liberal Center, and furious pips of protest from the Peace Movement") may step forward once again into the truly adventurous reality of human existence. Ours is a time, as Mailer sees it (in "The Ninth" of *The Presidential Papers*), in which that "rough beast" Yeats foresaw as slouching towards Bethlehem has been

> transported, modified, codified, and inserted into each of us by way of the popular arts, the social crafts, the political crafts, and the corporate techniques. It sits in the image of the commercials on television which use phallic and vaginal symbols to sell products which are otherwise useless for sex, it is heard in the jargon of educators, in the synthetic continuums of prose with which public-relations men learn to enclose the sense and smell of an event, it resides in the taste of frozen food, the pharmaceutical odor of tranquillizers, the planned obsolescence of automobiles, the lack of workmanship in the mass, it lives . . . in the sexual excess of lovers who love each other into apathy, it is the livid passion which takes us to sleeping pills, the mechanical action in every household appliance which breaks too soon, it vibrates in the sound of an air conditioner or the flicker of fluorescent lighting. And it proliferates in that new architecture which rests like an incubus upon the American landscape. . . .

Mailer's name for this disease which has slipped into our cells is Totalitarianism. And his central contention is that, when we are by way of being utterly strangled by social and moral systems so elaborately false their falsity can no longer even be precisely traced, then we must simply burst the belt—by searching out those extreme situations (of risk and danger) wherein we may at least recover the taste of our actual humanity. This is the way of the Hipster, of the "existential hero"—who dares to *descend* into "the destructive element," believing that there indeed it is that one's authenticity is to be found. When God and the Devil, in other words, are locked in mortal combat—when, that is, the forces which promote richness and abundance of human life are pitted against those which seek to flatten our world out into the standardized banalities of mass technocracy—we have no other choice but to face, as unblinkingly and courageously as we can, the "uninhabitable terrain of the absurd." And on that terrain "new circuits" must be made. It is such ideas as these—obviously not the ideas of a social scientist but the vital intuitions of a poetic intelligence—which are at the center of Mailer's essays in the late 1950s and early 1960s.

It seems clear, however, that in all the work which went into the *Advertisements*, *The Presidential Papers*, and *Cannibals and Christians* he was in effect (brilliant though much of it is) tiding over hard times until he could manage to produce a large work of fiction that would in some incandescent way present a major image of the "existential hero." And what he did finally manage in this connection was the bizarre and provocative novel of 1965, *An American Dream*.

\*      \*      \*

Not since *The Naked and the Dead* has one of Mailer's fictions received a generally favorable press; but none of his previous novels, not even *Barbary Shore*, had been so

badly treated as was the book of 1965. Very nearly everywhere it was declared to be something insufferably outrageous in its morality and ludicrously bungled in its
narrative art; and, at faculty parties on midwestern cam-
puses and in the journals of New York literati, one heard
that this oafish *belligérant* had irretrievably committed
himself to a degree of ethical and artistic idiosyncrasy
(hadn't he stabbed one of his wives?) that simply required
him to be immediately expelled from the circle of one's
attention. Every now and then American literary people
who smoke cigarettes and drink their daily portion of hard
liquor and invent their own sexual codes and own no
authority of either Church or Synagogue are seized by a
great feverish compulsion to establish their credentials,
after all, as persons thoroughly responsible and upright. It
is a strange proclivity, but one which (as sociologists of our
literary life may verify and study it) is recurrently felt—
and, in the winter and spring of 1965, Norman Mailer and
his book were its victims. Elizabeth Hardwick's notice in
*Partisan Review* declared the novel to be "a very dirty
book—dirty and extremely ugly"; Philip Rahv, in *The New
York Review of Books*, took its "excruciated sexology" to
be an indication of Mailer's having "repressed . . . his common sense as well as the moral side of his nature"; the
reviewer for *Harper's* thought the book might possibly be
considered "an obscene travesty of American life"; and so
the refrain went tiresomely on over the several weeks that
the work was being talked about in Sunday supplements
and magazines.

The immediate detail of Mailer's anecdote will no doubt
seem monstrous to the plain reader. Stephen Richards
Rojack—Harvard Phi Beta Kappa, winner of a D.S.C. in
World War II, ex-Congressman from New York, professor
of something called Existential Psychology in an unnamed
university in New York City (presumably Columbia), and

popular television pundit—is now, *nel mezzo del cammin,* at the end of the line. He is estranged and living apart from his rich and bitchy wife, the former Deborah Kelly (whom he met on a double date with Jack Kennedy, when they were both freshman Congressmen); he is head over heels in debt; and he is unable to bring to completion his long projected book. So, at a party being given by a friend one night, he feels impelled for a moment to hurl himself off the balcony of his friend's tenth-floor Sutton Place apartment. There was a full moon that night, and it seemed to be saying, "Come to me. Come now. Now!" But, in this moment, some "psychic bombardment" of the death impulse keeps him from going over the balustrade. And he rushes from his friend's apartment to Deborah's East River Drive duplex—a sinister "hot-house of flat velvet flowers" —where she, always "an artist with the needle," soon begins mockingly to speak of her current lovers. He strikes her, and she immediately charges "like a bull." In the struggle that ensues, one part of Rojack's mind says, "Hold back! you're going too far, hold back!"—but, as he tells us,

> some desire to go ahead not unlike the instant one comes in a woman against her cry that she is without protection came bursting with rage from out of me and my mind exploded in a fireworks of rockets, stars, and hurtling embers, the arm about her neck leaped against the whisper I could still feel murmuring in her throat, and *crack* I choked her harder, and *crack* I choked her again, and *crack* I gave her payment—never halt now— and *crack* the door flew open and the wire tore in her throat, and I was through the door, hatred passing from me in wave after wave. . . .

The murder completed, Rojack—not having "felt so nice since I was twelve"—decides not immediately to telephone the police; and, after adjusting his black knit tie, with "a good sound somewhere in [his] head," he goes downstairs to the bedroom of Deborah's German maid, Fräulein Ruta. He enters without knocking, and, finding her off in that autoerotic "bower of the libido where she was queen," he strips off his clothing and proceeds to satisfy her need, in the course of things even by buggery. Then, when this fancy game has been played out, he goes back up to Deborah's room, and, thinking that he ought to arrange a "suicide" before calling the police, he opens a window and flings her body over the ledge. Once the precinct station has been phoned and just before he leaves the apartment, as he brushes by Fräulein Ruta in the foyer, he is seized again "with a hopeless lust"—"thirty seconds was all I wanted"—and there is one last "bangeroo" in the hall.

The police view the dead woman's husband with suspicion, but, in the absence of any substantially incriminating evidence against him, Rojack is released after being questioned—whereupon he goes off to a nightclub with a blonde *chanteuse* named Cherry, whom he meets in the precinct station at the time of his interrogation. She, as it turns out, was formerly the mistress of the tycoon Barney Oswald Kelly, Deborah's father, by whom she became pregnant in Las Vegas. But, since Kelly's interest in Cherry proved fleeting, she arranged an abortion—as she also found it necessary to do when her affair with a Negro singer, Shago Martin, resulted in pregnancy. Cherry's journey through the world has, in short, been a difficult one, but she finds Rojack's "magic" irresistible: so, after their departure from the nightclub, she takes him to a tenement on the lower east side where, apart from her established residence, she keeps a room formerly occupied by a younger sister and where they make love. Rojack "had never moved so well," and Cherry has her first great, oceanic orgasm. These raptures are interrupted, however, by the sound of someone knocking on the door: it is Shago Martin, who, even though his affair with Cherry is over, is so angered by what he finds that he threatens Rojack with a drawn knife—which leads to a fight culminating in Shago's being badly beaten and thrown out into the street by Rojack.

At last Rojack receives word that the police have been directed to terminate their investigation of him and to close the case issuing from his wife's death. Suspecting that her father may have arranged this, he goes to Kelly's Waldorf Towers penthouse, where he is admitted by Fräulein Ruta, whom Kelly, as Rojack discovers, had placed in Deborah's apartment as a spy. But this is only the lesser of his discoveries. In the conversation with his father-in-law, he learns that Kelly had kept an incestuous relationship with his daughter since her early girlhood. And he in turn admits to Kelly that he killed Deborah. The air of the apartment becomes heavy with "a funk of gloom" and Rojack feels summoned outside to the terrace, feels summoned indeed to walk around its parapet. This he proceeds to do, hundreds of feet above the street below. Kelly attempts to push him off, with an umbrella of Shago Martin's that Rojack has brought with him, but Rojack manages to grip the umbrella and to jump down to the terrace floor in the nick of time. In a great rage, he beats Kelly into unconsciousness with the umbrella before departing.

He then returns to Cherry's tenement room, where he finds her dying from a brutal beating administered as an act of revenge by one of Shago Martin's friends. The police on the scene tell him that Shago himself has just been killed in Morningside Park.

And all this occurs within a matter of thirty-two hours.

At the end, the Epilogue finds Rojack at the gambling tables in Las Vegas. And just before striking out for the

territory ahead—Guatemala and Yucatán—he telephones
Cherry, who says that things are "swell" and that "Marilyn
says to say hello."

Such, in barest outline, is the fantastic romp that the
novel recounts. It is, of course, an utterly implausible
romance, something grotesque and nasty indeed beyond
words, if it be considered simply in the terms of its
sequence of events and as if this narrative constituted a
purportedly realistic rendering of a moral situation. But
one might have expected readers of far less sophistication
than Elizabeth Hardwick and Philip Rahv immediately to
discern, from the wildly baroque language of Rojack's
recital, that this book—about a man who believes that
"magic, dread, and the perception of death [are] the roots
of motivation"—is primarily an essay in conjuration and
warlockry which wants, as its title suggests, to explore that
"subterranean river of untapped, ferocious, lonely and
romantic desires, that concentration of ecstasy and violence which is the dream life of the nation" (*The Presidential Papers*). We move, to be sure, in and out of the
myriad worlds of New York City, and the inattentive
reader may be hoodwinked into supposing that the ordinary conventions of social narrative are at work, for the
characters have jobs and make love and sometimes collide
with the agencies of local law enforcement. But, of course,
as alleged occurrence, the whole fable is manifestly ridicu-
lous: Rojack speaks at a certain point of having lost faith
"in a world which believed in the *New York Times*," and
so indeed it might be said of the novel in which he holds
the central place, that, for the sake of its myth, it asks us
to consent momentarily to a "teleological suspension" of
all those ethical considerations which normally prevail in
that world where we soberly read the *New York Times*
over our breakfast coffee.

*An American Dream* needs to be read in the closest

relation to the testimony presented in *Advertisements for Myself,* in *The Presidential Papers* and in *Cannibals and Christians,* as it also requires finally to be considered, in its basic emphasis, organically of a piece with what has been seen to be the developing logic of the vision controlling Mailer's entire effort as a novelist, from *The Naked and the Dead* to *The Deer Park.* His subject remains what it had been throughout all the previous years of his career as a writer—namely, the burdens which we bear now in America by reason of "the complex fate" which is our historical inheritance. And the meditation in this vein which resulted in the novel of 1965 had been fiercely shaped by the pressure of his deepening conviction—brilliantly set forth in his essays of the early sixties—that a terrible "plague" has slipped into the cells and bloodstream of American life, a plague which he named Totalitarianism and whose radicality appeared to make the rituals and stratagems of conventional politics no longer pertinent to the actualities of our condition. The usual distinctions of party and program struck him as having quite lost any genuine significance. For whether you turned to George Romney (who "looked like a handsome version of Boris Karloff") or to Nelson Rockefeller (whose "eyes . . . had the distant lunar glow of the small sad eyes you see in a caged champanzee or gorilla") or to Lyndon Johnson (a Texas gambler with "the vanity of a modern dictator," the very triumph of the scientific spirit with his nice capacity for telling you that "yesterday we knocked off ninety-four gooks" in Vietnam), the conclusion could hardly be avoided that the new men at the helm were people whose mediocrity or cupidity had the effect of bringing to an end the "art of the possible" in our public life. So, after the death of John Kennedy—whose thousand days in the White House had brought a brief season of hope—Mailer's decision was that any relevant plotting of a decent prospect must move beyond the customary frames of social tactics, must begin indeed with the notion on which (as he declared in *The Presidential Papers*) a truly "existential politics" is based, "that we live out our lives wandering among mysteries, and can construct the few hypotheses by which we guide ourselves only by drawing into ourselves the instinctive logic our inner voice tells us is true to the relations *between* mysteries."

Now, in the American world daily reported on in the *New York Times*, Stephen Richards Rojack has already prior to the beginning of his narrative realized the nation's characteristic dream of success. He was accorded a hero's recognition in the Second World War; he is married to a beautiful and wealthy socialite; he has achieved distinction of status as a scholar in the university community; he has managed successfully to market his scholarship on a popular New York television show; he has had a varied and triumphant sexual career; he has even prospered in the realm of practical politics, for not only has he served in the Congress of the United States but it is hinted that he might have chosen to go on to the halls of the Senate. In the Third of his *Presidential Papers* Mailer speaks of America as having been "the country in which the dynamic myth of the Renaissance—that every man was potentially extraordinary—knew its most passionate persistence." And in no particular has Rojack had occasion to find any fraudulence in this myth, for he has had love and adventure and professional success and public recognition and has enjoyed all the sweets promised by Horatio Alger. But his achievement of the American Dream has brought him no felicity or blessedness, and, as he tells us at the very outset, he has "come to the end of a very long street": he constantly feels that he is about to be deprived of what he calls his "center," and he is a man who, gazing down into the unfulfilled possibility of his existence, is possessed by

that terrible emptiness which Kierkegaard called "dread."
So, like Tom o' Bedlam he feels himself

> . . . summoned . . . to Tourney
> Ten leagues beyond
> The wide world's end. . . .

And he enters "the mysteries of murder, suicide, incest,
orgy, orgasm and Time"—which is to say that, in his quest
for authenticity of being, he becomes a "psychic outlaw."

What needs to be understood, however, is that in Mailer's universe the concept of the psychic outlaw is a radical
metaphor which speaks simply of the deviateness that, in a
standardized mass society, will inevitably seem to be exemplified by any man who is genuinely committed to the
autonomy of his own selfhood and who has, therefore, the
courage to say "I." Kierkegaard, in the little book called
*The Present Age* which he wrote in the winter of 1846,
was already a century ago remarking the rapidity with
which the crowd was becoming the fundamental form of
human existence in the modern world. Rather than undertaking candidly to face the naked reality of their human
condition, men, he said, are more and more instead forming a committee—and "in the end the whole age becomes a
committee," the world being invaded by what he called
"the public . . . a kind of gigantic something, an abstract
and deserted void which is everything and nothing." Nor
was Kierkegaard by any means the last to rail against the
"levelling" tendencies of modern society whereby the individual is submerged in an impersonal social collective.
From de Tocqueville (Kierkegaard's French contemporary)
to Gabriel Marcel and from Nietzsche to Jaspers and Or-
tega and Berdyaev, a similar testimony has been one of the
great refrains in cultural critique of the last hundred years
and has deeply entered into the lore of the intellectual
universe by which Norman Mailer was formed. So he says,

in the way of a brisk and striking trope, the man who steps aside from the collectivist drift of American life and who proceeds himself to assume the burden of his own humanity will be a "psychic outlaw." And the great example of such a man that he offers in his fiction is the hero of *An American Dream.*

Now the metaphor of the psychic outlaw is but the "armature" of the larger metaphor represented by the entire anecdote which Rojack recounts. Which is to say that it is not the intention of the anecdote to solicit a credent response to its details, for the anecdote—as the consistently larky and playful tone of its recital emphatically indicates—is only so much moonshine: it is a fantastic extravaganza not simply narrated but also invented by Rojack, as a device wherewith to suggest how bracing and renovative it may be, in a bullying world, for a man (unredeemed by the American Dream) simply to release and revel in the sheer riot and fecundity of his own imaginative powers. And the marvel is that, among the numerous commentators on the book, it is Leo Bersani alone who has had the wit to see this with effective clarity. Even those who have attempted to mount some sort of defense of Mailer against the philistines have, most of them, treated the novel as a kind of conventional essay in existentialist nihilism that proposes an ethic of "courage" for which the testing ground is violence—but done, of course, they say in effect, with a *brio* so extraordinary as to permit us to make allowances for its moral obscurantism. Rojack is a man on whom life is closing in, a man who had long known murder to be hiding within his anguished frustration. So, in "the existentialist moment," when he is confronted by a malevolent wife—the Great Bitch who "delivers extermination to any bucko brave enough to take carnal knowledge of her" and who irradiates from every pore of her body that "sullen poisonous fire" by which he feels himself about to be destroyed—he chokes her to death and thus, having gotten murder and death out of his system, he makes his way back (with the help of Cherry) to *la vita nuova*. The novel is taken to be, in short, an essay in the psychology of the extreme situation and, as a piece of psychological research, is talked about in the terms made familiar by similar discussions of Stendhal, Dostoievski, Gide, and Camus. But nothing could be more irrelevant, for the novel's anecdote, as Mr. Bersani carefully observes, is, in Rojack's telling of it, nothing more than "a brilliant and difficult trick" which gives Mailer's protagonist a chance

> to entertain the most extravagant fantasies and hallucinations in order to change their affective coefficient. By taking the risk of abandoning himself to the fantastic suggestiveness of every person, every object, every smell encountered during the thirty-two hours he writes about, Rojack discovers fantasy as a source of imaginative richness in himself instead of fearing it as an ominous signal from mysterious, external powers. He moves, in other words, from fantasy as a psychological illusion about the world to the use of fantasy as a somewhat self-conscious but exuberant display of his own inventive powers.[10]

What is decisive in this connection is that aspect of the novel which is most essentially an affair of *l'écriture*, of its writing. For it is just on this level, in the prankish exuberance of the speech that Rojack employs (with the extravagance of a Virgil Fox doing a Bach fugue), that Mailer is to be found not only making game of his anecdote but also disclosing the primary motive at work in his hero. Here, for example, is a part of Rojack's account of an occasion

[10]Leo Bersani, "Mailer and His Critics: The Interpretation of Dreams," *Partisan Review*, 32, no. 4 (Fall, 1965):606.

during the War when he and his platoon suddenly encountered a German machine gun unit:

> The grenades went off somewhere between five and ten
> yards over each machine gun, *blast, blast,* like a boxer's
> tattoo, one-two, and I was exploded in the butt from a
> piece of my own shrapnel, whacked with a delicious
> pain clean as a mistress' sharp teeth going "Yummy" in
> your rump, and then the barrel of my carbine swung
> around like a long fine antenna and pointed itself at the
> machine-gun hole on my right where a great bloody
> sweet German face, a healthy spoiled overspoiled young
> beauty of a face, mother-love all over its making, posses-
> sor of that overcurved mouth which only great fat sweet
> young faggots can have when their rectum is tuned and
> entertained from adolescence on, came crying, sliding,
> smiling up over the edge of the hole, "Hello death!"
> blood and mud like the herald of sodomy upon his
> chest, and I pulled the trigger as if I were squeezing the
> softest breast of the softest pigeon which ever flew, still
> a woman's breast takes me now and then to the pigeon
> on that trigger, and the shot cracked like a birth twig
> across my palm, *whop!* and the round went in at the
> base of his nose and spread and I saw his face sucked in
> backward upon the gouge of the bullet, he looked
> suddenly like an old man, toothless, sly, reminiscent of
> lechery. Then he whimpered *"Mutter,"* one yelp from
> the first memory of the womb, and down he went into
> his own blood. . . .

Or, again, after cracking Deborah's throat, he goes into her
bathroom to wash his hands and adjust his tie, and then,
on returning to her bedroom, this, as he tells us, is how she
looked:

> She was bad in death. A beast stared back at me. Her
> teeth showed, the point of light in her eye was violent,

and her mouth was open. It looked like a cave. I could hear some wind which reached down to the cellars of a sunless earth. A little line of spit came from the corner of her mouth, and at an angle from her nose one green seed had floated its small distance on an abortive rill of blood.

And, at a later point, as he views her body amidst the stench of the morgue's antiseptic and deodorant, he tells us that he "caught.... a clear view of one green eye staring open, hard as marble, dead as the dead eye of a fish, and her poor face swollen, her beauty gone obese."

Or, again, here is Rojack's description of Cherry singing in her nightclub on the evening of their first meeting:

I was watching her foot beat the rhythm. She was wearing sandals which exposed her toes, and she had painted her nails. I was taken with this vanity, I was absorbed with it, for like most attractive women, her toes were the ugliest part of her body. Not ugly exactly, not deformed, but certainly too large. Her big toe was round, round as a half dollar, and larger than a quarter—it was one round greedy self-satisfied digit, and the four little toes were not so little either, each of them round balls, each of them much larger in their pads than the size of the nail might justify, so that one had to peek at five sensuous, even piggish, but most complacent little melons of flesh surrounding five relatively tiny toenails, each broader than they were long, which depressed me. She had the short broad foot of that very practical kind of woman who has time to buy the groceries and time to jazz the neighbor next door....

Now it is in such passages as these—which give a kind of sunny vibrancy to every page of the book—it is just here, in the wonderfully uninhibited vivaciousness of the language of Rojack's narrative, that the moral drama of the

novel lies. It is not, in other words, his deeds—which are a
tall story he playfully fabricates—but his rhetoric that
establishes Rojack as a psychic outlaw, that proves him
indeed to have moved out into a world beyond that of the
*New York Times.* For his is the language of a man who
dares to give himself with utter abandon to the richness
and idiosyncrasy of his own perceptions. And it is just in
this way that he presents in his very outrageousness something like a mythic example of that compactness of identity which alone is calculated finally to subvert the "totalitarianism" of a technocratic culture.

So it is a trifle absurd for certain of Norman Mailer's
critics, with some manual of style in hand, to reproach him
for the ways in which he twists and bends his medium in
*An American Dream.* Rojack's similes, as a case in point,
are often very loose-jointed indeed. He tells us, for example, how Cherry, when singing in her nightclub, on the
words *sleepy garden walls* "struck five perfect notes, five,
like the five bells of an angel come to the wake of a
bomb." And, when they first make love, he says that, after
paying their devotions in some church no larger than
themselves, they "traveled . . . through some midnight of
inner space" and then "reached into some middle ground
of a race"—"like bicycle riders caught in the move of lap
after lap around a track. . . ." Or he says that in the living
room of Kelly's penthouse there was "a presence . . . like
the command of a dead pharaoh." This kind of figure pops
out at us from nearly every paragraph of the book, and
numerous dons (who ought to know better) and Sunday
supplement hacks have scored Mailer off about how
"badly" he's writing here, about the similes that cannot be
parsed. But, as Wilfrid Sheed has remarked (in his *New
York Times Book Review* notice of *Cannibals and Christians,* 21 August 1966), Mailer commands, in his immense
sophistication about the gesticulatory possibilities of our

language, "more sheer literary taste than a whole year's supply of the Whatsitsname Review": he can write his prose, as Mr. Sheed rightly says, "as well or as badly as he wants to: clogged and turgid, clean and graceful." He knows, in other words, what he is up to, and what he is up to in the amazingly brilliant conceit woven around Stephen Richards Rojack is not so much a novel as a sort of prose poem whose purpose it is to hint at how a self that has not been served well by the American Dream may remake itself—not by the performance of such deeds as the anecdote comically attributes to its protagonist but by paying the strictest heed to the rhythms of its own interior life. And the result is a beautifully rendered book that asks for the kind of attention required by only a few works of recent fiction.

*        *        *

It was immediately apparent at the end of the summer of 1967, when the novel that followed *An American Dream* made its appearance, that in *Why Are We in Vietnam?* Mailer had created a fiction whose mode of statement, in its obliqueness and indirection, was no less elaborate than that of his previous novel. Indeed, this remarkable book made fully evident what ought already to have been suggested by *An American Dream,* that Mailer's progress had followed a route by which he had come now no longer to have any commitment at all to the practice of traditional novelistic realism. There could no longer be any mistaking it, that, like many of the most interesting novelists of our period, he had lost all interest in the Balzacian aim, of enlarging the common stock of information about matters of public fact. It was now clear that no longer did he want so much to create new stories as to explore new rhythms of feeling and perception, of self-consciousness and moral energy. Not for him, therefore, the cultivated, standard parlance of a Styron or an Updike—but, rather, it was in a swift vernacular heavily laced with a slangy wit and obscenity that he had found a language appropriate to the research he wanted to conduct into the turmoil and astonishment that belong to the American adventure in our time.

On the occasion of their Christmas meetings in 1965, when the scholars had persuaded him to address a meeting of the Modern Language Association—having expected to be titillated by the high jinks of a preposterous jester, but getting instead a brilliant discourse on the various modes of American fiction (later published in *Commentary*)— Mailer expressed his own judgment that at no point in this century had realistic fiction (whether in the manner of Dreiser or of Edith Wharton) succeeded in rendering the full actuality of American life. This, he suggested, is why in our own period the novel has given "up any desire to be a creation equal to the phenomenon of the country itself." Instead, each writer chooses now to make his own "separate peace," attempting

> merely . . . to give life to some microcosm in American life, some metaphor—in the sense that a drop of water is a metaphor of the seas, or a hair of the beast is for some a metaphor of the beast. . . .

Hemingway, he said, wrote not about the beast but "about the paw of the beast," and "Faulkner about the dreams of the beast."[11] And, as we may be reminded by the wonderfully artful insinuativeness of his novel of 1967, so indeed

[11]Norman Mailer, "Modes and Mutations: Quick Comments on the Modern American Novel," *Commentary*, 41, no. 3 (March, 1966):39. This address, in somewhat revised form, also appears in *Cannibals and Christians*.

has it increasingly been the tendency of Mailer himself to deal with "the beast" as metaphorist, as a specialist not so much in chronicle and narrative as in those flashing analogies and that verbal magic which may, together, convey a deeper perception of the beast's dark interior.

There is, of course, a narrative line in *Why Are We in Vietnam?*, though it is something quite as deceptive as the narrative recounted in *An American Dream,* for this book, finally, is no more an essay in pastoral (as its narrative at first makes it seem) than the book of 1965 is any sort of "swinging" essay in pornography. But its external surface presents it as—like Mark Twain's *Huckleberry Finn* and the Nick Adams stories in Hemingway's *In Our Time* and Faulkner's *The Bear*—a tale dealing with a youth's *rite de passage* in the setting of a wilderness far removed from the counterfeit world of civilized society. The narrator of the story is a lewd-talking eighteen-year-old stud, Ranald Jethroe Jellicoe Jethroe, the son of a Dallas millionaire, Rutherford David Jethroe Jellicoe Jethroe, who manufactures a plastic cigarette filter—"the filter with the purest porosity of purpose"—that "traps all the nicotine, sucks up every bit of your spit," and, without being guaranteed to do so, "also causes cancer of the lip." Young Jethroe thinks that "there's a tape recorder in Heaven for each of us . . . taking it all down": so he *broadcasts*—styling himself as "disc jockey to the world," calling himself "D.J." And, on the eve of his departure for military duty in Vietnam (along with his closest chum, Gottfried Hyde Junior, nicknamed "Tex," the son of a Dallas mortician), the harangue of which he delivers himself—as "wandering troubadour" with a new program for America on "how to live in this Electrolux Edison world"—concerns an Alaskan hunting expedition for grizzly bear on which, two years before, he and Tex had accompanied the elder Jethroe (Big Daddy, or Rusty as he's known by his friends), along with two of Rusty's corporation flunkies ("call them Medium Asshole Pete and Medium Asshole Bill—M.A. Pete . . . and M.A. Bill"), their professional guide Big Luke Fellinka, his Indian assistant, Ollie Totem Head Water Beaver, and their crew.

These "Dallasassians"—which is D.J.'s name for the residents of the city in which John Kennedy's skull was shattered—flew up for their safari from Dallas to Alaska's Brooks Mountain Range, and much of D.J.'s narrative is given over to an account of the hunt for the great grizzlies amid the remote northern snows. He warns us that he "suffers from one great American virtue, or maybe it's a disease or ocular dysfunction—D.J. sees right through shit." And thus he does not conceal the terrible brutality with which his corporation-executive father and Rusty's stooges invade the Range. Over so long a time has this wilderness been violated by ravenous hunters and so often have the bear been simply wounded and then pitilessly left to thrash about in their agony that their hatred of the human presence has now become a flinty, demoniac malevolence, and Big Ollie warns his clients that "animal no wild no more, now crazy." But the Medium Assholes simply laugh, "each of them separately and respectively like Henry Fonda and Jimmy Stewart," and Rusty is unimpressed, for, as he says, ". . . the bear is the integral part of this expedition." He's engaged Big Luke, the finest guide in Alaska; he's brought along the finest gear that money can buy; and he has no intention of going back to Dallas without a bear. He's come up on a Class A trip, "a Charley Wilson, John Glenn, Arnold Palmer, Gary Cooper kind of trip, next thing in top category you might say to a Jackie Kennedy Bobby Kennedy Ethel and the kids' trip"—and he doesn't mean to settle for a deer. "I'm a stubborn Texas son of a bitch," he says. So he engages a helicopter to stalk his prey and to round up the animals within easy firing distance of the party's huge Magnum rifles, so powerful as very nearly to be capable of delivering "a grenade and bullet all in one sweet cartridge package . . . which will drop a grizzly if it hits him in the toe." But Rusty intends to aim not for the toe but the shoulder:

> "Right," says Rusty. . . . "Break the shoulder bone, and they can't run. Sure. That's where I want my power. Right there. . . . Maybe a professional hunter takes pride in dropping an animal by picking him off in a vital spot—but I like the feeling that if I miss a vital area I still can count on the big impact knocking them down, killing them by the total impact, shock! it's like aerial bombardment in the last Big War. . . . It's just like if you get in a fight with a fellow, you're well advised to destroy him half to death. If y'get him down, use your shoe on his face, employ your imagination, give him a working-over, hard to believe, but often enough that man is your friend afterward. . . .

Yet, despite the ferocious technology he turns loose on his quarry, Rusty is not lucky. Young Tex gets a bear, and so does one of the Medium Assholes (M.A. Pete)—but the kingpin is without his prize. After a time, he and D.J. desert the others and set off on their own, "like two combat wolves, eyes to the left, eyes to the right . . . their steps keen off each little start of sound. . . ." And, after several hours, they find a trail which brings them suddenly around the side of a ledge, into the presence of a great giant who comes "at them on the heuuuuuu of the cry, two red coal little eyes of fire, wall of fur coming fast as a locomotive." The bear is shot but not killed, and they follow him into the dense foliage. They come upon him, dying. D.J. touches his rifle "slightly with a little salute" and starts walking toward him, as he and the bear exchange wordless messages with their eyes. But before he can fire, as he has won the right to do by coming into a proximity which Rusty hasn't dared, Rusty from a safe distance shoots, and the grizzly goes "up to death in one last paroxysm." When they get back to their camp and Rusty in the presence of the others claims the bear as his own, D.J.'s only comment—to us—is "Whew. Final end of love of one son for one father."

The next morning, disgusted by the corruption in his father that has for him at last been *proved* by the fraudulence with which on the evening before Rusty had claimed himself to have taken the bear ("Yeah, I guess it's mine. . . ."), D.J. sets out with Tex, before dawn, for a trek through the woods. In a way very much reminiscent of the ceremony enacted by Ike McCaslin in Faulkner's *The Bear*, they leave their guns behind, their knives, even their compasses and sleeping bags, and head out into the wilderness. Their spirits are deeply touched by "something in the radiance of the North," and, unafraid, they move way up into the Range beyond the timber line—where, far away from all the improbities of men, they spend a night together under the northern stars, achieving some new unspeakable sense of the strange and beautiful mystery of their humanity, before going back down to the camp and to "the same specific mix of mixed old shit."

Then, D.J.'s narrative of that hunt being ended, on the last page of the novel—on the evening of a party being given in his honor in Rusty's "Dallas ass manse"—we hear the first mention of Vietnam, when the young Disc Jockey, in his final "beeping out," tells us that ". . . tomorrow Tex and me, we're off to see the wizard in Vietnam. . . . So, ass-head America contemplate your butt. . . . This is D.J., Disc Jockey to America turning off. Vietnam, hot damn."

Now this Arcadian narrative, with its account of a ritual of purification occurring under the Northern lights and in the unpolluted air of the Arctic wilderness, is wonderfully sustained by an extraordinary energy of inventiveness and by Mailer's genius for rendering the immediacies of sensory experience, in all their thickness and particularity. The novel has its story, for it relates the tale of a hunt which becomes for a boy on the threshold of manhood the occasion for a time of testing and for a great shock of recognition; and, on this level, the book achieves a lyrical beauty that does not embarrass the pastoral tradition of Hemingway and Faulkner which it obviously wants to invoke. But, as in *An American Dream,* it is not so much in the recounted narrative as in the *voice* which tells the story that we find the real center of the novel's interest. For it is in the militantly scatological rhetoric and the high-pitched, outraged intonations of this young monologist, "D.J." Jethroe, that the novel intends us to find the answer to the question which it poses in its title; and it is D.J.'s voice that we find even more commanding than the story which the voice relates.

Here is an American boy who, with his gift for seeing "right through shit," has had to confront the fact that his own father, Rutherford David Jethroe Jellicoe Jethroe, is nothing more than a consummate instance of that mindless, dehumanized emptiness marking the conventional corporation executive—looking, to be sure, "like a high-breed crossing between Dwight D. Eisenhower and Henry Cabot Lodge," with eyes that have "a friendly twinkle," but, nevertheless, with nothing more than "a plastic asshole . . . in his brain":

> I mean that's what you get when you look into Rusty's eyes. You get voids, man, and gleams of yellow fire—the woods is burning somewhere in his gray matter—and then there's marble aisles, better believe it, fifty thousand fucking miles of marble floor down those eyes and you got to walk over that to get to The Man.

It is in this man's house that D.J., as his son, has been fated to live, and what Mailer says of himself as a tenant in the disordered House of our American Republic might well be applied to the hero of *Why Are We in Vietnam?*. He says of the role assigned himself in his account (*The Armies of the Night*) of the quixotic march on the Pentagon undertaken in October of 1967 by pacifists protesting the Vietnam war:

> It is fitting that any ambiguous comic hero of such a history should be not only off very much to the side of the history, but that he should be an egotist of the most startling misproportions, outrageously and often unhappily self-assertive, yet in command of a detachment classic in severity.

And so it is also with young D.J.. Splendidly uninhibited in his egotism, he says to us quite bluntly: "You're contending with a genius, D.J. is his name, only American alive who could outtalk Cassius Clay. . . ." And it is just the gay nonchalance of his self-love which enables him in his father's house to stand "very much to the side," to "command . . . a detachment [almost] classic in severity," and to face unblinkingly the fact that his father is the very "cream of corporation corporateness," that Rusty lives in "this Electrolux Edison world" as one who is "all programmed out," the great "plastic asshole installed in his brain" excreting nothing more than "his corporate management of thoughts." So D.J.'s exacting conscience requires him to think of his father as incarnating the spirit of a system—the sterile, totalitarian system of corporation life—that stains the soul and that promises to take possession of the country. "He's a real pig, man!"—this "highbreed crossing between Dwight D. Eisenhower and Henry Cabot Lodge," who "gives contribs" to the ADA ("under the table") and the John Birch Society and who holds membership in "the Second Congregated Anglo Episcopal and Conjoint Presbyterian Clutch and Methodist Church," along with his enrollments in innumerable country clubs and credit societies (Diners' Club, Carte Blanche, American Express, etc.).

So it is no wonder that D.J., though he's frank to say that he's never read Kierkegaard (not Fyodor Kierkegaard, "you assholes"—but "*Sören* Kierkegaard"), is yet "up tight with the concept of dread." For "Big Daddy" *is* the country, and this is what his narrative is, most fundamentally, about—Big Daddy *as* the country. D.J., with his lively imagination of the old America and its pioneering adventuresomeness, has a great sense of what we *might* have been and of what he and Rusty *could* have recovered together in the northern snows of the Brooks Range—but, there (again to borrow the language of *The Armies of the Night*), the fever for adventure and travel which had always been "in the American blood . . . [was found to have] left the blood, it was in the cells, the cells traveled, and the cells were as insane as Grandma with orange hair."

Thus it is that D.J.'s narrative, in focusing on the barbarism that Rusty augurs, tells us why we are in Vietnam. That is to say, we are committed to the wild and shameful misadventure in Southeast Asia because the country itself is mad. In John Aldridge's decoding of the parable, the forces that drive Rusty Jethroe

> . . . to become a promiscuous slayer of animals are the same as those that have driven the nation into promiscuous military aggressiveness. . . . At some point in Rusty's development his native pioneer impulses toward adventure and self-challenge, impulses which might once have found an outlet in the testing hazards of the frontier, have been blocked in him and become the poison of his psychic life. . . . Hence, his existence has

degenerated into a series of small, vicious, power-seeking
conquests of the animal and business world. . . . He
therefore has never discovered his potentialities for life.
He knows only the experience of dread.[12]

And this is what the novel is about—a certain death in the
national soul of which Vietnam is the great symptom. But
the drama of the book is in the beautifully cadenced and
hilarious obscenities of the young hero whose rage at the
environing wilderness of the country's life makes for one
of the great poetries of speech in modern American fiction.

Yet John Aldridge's argument, that in D.J. Mailer presents a significant alternative to the rampant barbarism
instanced by Rusty, cannot finally be sustained. For, on
close examination, the catharsis which Tex and D.J. are
supposed to have undergone in the snow capped highlands
of Alaska appears to be something very ambiguous indeed.
On that night up in the wilds of the Brooks Mountain
Range, after the two boys had bedded down together,
D.J.—electrified by the eerie vastness and the luminous
beauty of the northern lights—had begun to feel, deeply
stirring within himself, an insistently sexual longing for his
companion.[13]  "For the lights were talking to them,
and . . . were saying that there was something up here, and
it was really here, yeah God was here, and He was real and
no man was He, but a beast . . . [with a] secret call: come

12John W. Aldridge, "From Vietnam to Obscenity," *Harper's Magazine*, 236, no. 1413 (February, 1968):94.

13This episode does seem to have been somewhat willfully intro-
duced, and one wonders to what extent Mailer may have been
prompted by some odd caprice deliberately to shape his fable into
conformity with the version of *Huckleberry Finn* put forward in
Leslie Fiedler's famous essay "Come Back to the Raft Ag'in, Huck
Honey!" (*Partisan Review*, 15, no. 6 [June, 1948]:664-71).

to me." So all at once D.J. began to feel that, somehow, he and Tex might become one with this great beast through an act of love: he "knew he could make a try to prong Tex . . . and he was hard as a hammer at the thought and ready to give off sparks. . . ." But when he reached out to touch his friend, he found himself unexpectedly facing an antagonist, for Tex was not prepared to allow him to assume the male role: and thus, suddenly, there was

> murder between them under all friendship . . . and they hung there each of them on the knife of the divide in all conflict of lust to own the other yet in fear of being killed by the other and as the hour went by and the lights shifted, something in the radiance of the North went into them, and owned their fear, some communion of telepathies and new powers, and they were twins, never to be near as lovers again, but killer brothers, owned by something, prince of darkness, lord of light, they did not know. . . .

And it was in this tremulous moment of suppressed excitement and strain that D.J. heard the message of that great beast who is God and who said, "Go out and kill—fulfill my will, go and kill." D.J., in other words, has not kept off as much to the side of his father as he may think, and his detachment from Rusty's world is not altogether "classic in severity." Indeed, so deeply touched has he in fact been by that world that in this penultimate moment he is by way of deciding that "the center of things is insane . . . insane with force," with the kind of aggressive, exploitative force represented by his corporation-executive father. And one suspects that he felt a kind of confirmation of the beast's message not only in the violence his father had brought into those northern woods but also in the violence he had observed as a part of the very landscape itself—in the spectacle, for example, of a bear tearing open a live caribou calf to devour her entrails and then, for the sheer fun of it, ripping her to pieces and evacuating his bowels around the dead body. Even in this remote Arctic region, there was "madness in the air": so, drunk with "the essential animal insanity of things," D.J. and Tex, tuned in to the murmurs of God Himself, made a pact that night: "each bit a drop of blood from his own finger and touched them across and met, blood to blood, while the lights pulsated and glow of Arctic night was on the snow, and the deep beast whispering Fulfill my will, go forth and kill. . . ."

Then, at the end, two years later, we are gathered in the dining room of Rusty's "Dallas ass manse" for a celebrative occasion: D.J. and Tex are to be off the next morning for their Asian adventure. As D.J. says with enormous relish, in the final line of the novel, "Vietnam, hot damn"—for now, at last, he is about to go forth to fulfill the will of the Beast. In short, not even this boy who has a certain capacity for seeing "right through shit" escapes affliction by the disease which has slipped into the cells of the nation.

It is a profoundly disheartened conclusion, and, given the degree to which Mailer's disappointment with America has intensified itself to the point of becoming a veritably cosmic pessimism, the amazement is that he does, nevertheless, in the extraordinary vibrancy of the novel's language, manage to keep that jauntiness of tone which he chooses as his way of facing the human situation.

\*      \*      \*

The buoyant cheerfulness and good humor by which, despite its daunting conclusions, *Why Are We in Vietnam?* is marked are very much in evidence in Mailer's books of the last few years, even in his book of 1970, *The Prisoner of Sex*, his response to the bad-tempered attack leveled at him by the chief theorist of the new feminism, Kate Millett, in her manifesto of the same year, *Sexual Politics*. The author of *The Armies of the Night* and *Miami and the Siege of Chicago* (his account of the Republican and Democratic national conventions of 1968) is, indeed, a "smiling public man"—a "public man," of course, because like Whitman he chooses to address all the great public occasions of his period of American history (whether it be World War II, the Korean War, McCarthyism, the assassination of John Kennedy, or the whole issue of Vietnam) and because, with his extraordinary gift for self-advertisement, he has already become, in early middle age, a sort of monument on the American scene of the present time; but "smiling," because, for all his exasperation with the country for which he keeps an inordinate affection, he simply cannot contain his need for exultation.

But Mailer's *joie de vivre* is not sanctioned by his "philosophy": it is not a natural consequence of his social researches, of his moral and political doctrine, or of his highly idiosyncratic "theology," for on these levels his vision of the world has grown steadily darker over the past twenty years. On the contrary, one feels that the vivaciousness and gaiety that make Norman Mailer so endearing a presence in cultural life today represent an effervescence of spirit prompted by nothing more than the irresistibility of the man's impulse simply to revel in the astonishing prodigality of his own gifts as a writer. And this is, of course, what he most fundamentally is—not a seer, not any sort of political tactician, not a demagogue, but one whose vocation it is to supervise language in ways that will invigorate the imagination of the people of his age. Nor has Mailer ever for a moment failed to remember what his true office is. During the past decade he has, to be sure, undertaken numerous excursions into various areas of so-

cial and political action—but, always, one feels the guiding
principle of these involvements to have been something
like the principle subscribed to by young Lieutenant Hearn
in *The Naked and the Dead*, that authenticity of response
to the pressures of events is a matter of "style." For,
invariably, these sorties, whether into the thickets of the
peace movement or the Black insurgency or a New York
mayoralty campaign, strike us as feinting strategems in an
enterprise ultimately calculated to imply how the self—by
some new gesture of *style*—may overmaster what is oppres-
sively abstract and impersonal in the public life of the age.
Thus it is that this unmanageable chameleon would present, through the agency of the word, a redeeming model
of freedom. And, as impresario of a language appropriate
to freemen, his never-ending surprise at the marvelous feats
of which he proves himself capable so fills him with delight
that his voice is witty and exultant, even when the facts it
is reporting are dark and ominous.

Indeed, in his recent journalism as in his recent fiction—
in *The Armies of the Night, Miami and the Siege of
Chicago, St. George and the Godfather,*—it is *the man
speaking* who makes these books so richly human and so
memorable. In *The Armies of the Night,* as he describes his
participation in the march on the Pentagon in the autumn
of 1967, he refers to himself in the third person, as
"Mailer," and the character he allows this figure is sometimes that of a zany punchinello and sometimes that of the
legendary celebrity of American letters, sometimes that of
an "absolute egomaniac," or a "snob of the worst sort," or
a sort of swaggering bantam bent on pushing his way
through the crowd to the foremost place. And always the
voice one hears is at once insistent, assertive, pugnacious,
and humorously mocking and parodistic of itself. "Like
most New Yorkers," he says, "he usually felt small in
Washington. The capital invariably seemed to take the

measure of men like him." But he is unintimidated. On his first evening in town, at a party being given by "an attractive liberal couple" for other "liberal technologues" and for some of the more culturally prestigious people who have gathered for the weekend, he notices "the scent of the void which comes off the pages of a Xerox copy." Nor, as he is leaving the party, does he have any hesitancy about appropriating a coffee mug and filling it with bourbon. And immediately afterward, having had a good deal of that bourbon, at the first rally he addresses in a sleazy old movie house engaged for the occasion, he attempts—before being shushed up by the master of ceremonies and his fellow-speakers—to regale his audience with an account of how he missed the urinal in the men's room downstairs and wet the floor.

The pace of the narrative is rapid. But its tone suddenly changes for a moment to something quite different when, as he senses in the poet Robert Lowell (who is also on the platform) a sad disapproval of his antics, he thinks

> ... bitter words he would not say: "You, Lowell, beloved poet of many, what do you know of the dirt and dark deliveries of the necessary? What do you know of dignity hard-achieved, and dignity lost through innocence, and dignity lost by sacrifice for a cause one cannot name. What do you know about getting fat against your will, and turning into a clown of an arriviste baron when you would rather be an eagle or a count, or rarest of all, some natural aristocrat from these damned democratic states. . . . How dare you condemn me! . . . . How dare you scorn the explosive I employ?"

And it is with a similarly disarming candor that the protagonist measures himself in relation not only to Lowell but also to his other literary confreres—Dwight MacDonald,

Paul Goodman—who have come down from New York for the march. But it is especially on Lowell that he lingers, apparently sensing in his patrician hauteur some indefinable challenge that demands to be met (by a boy from a middle-class Jewish family in Brooklyn). As he looks at this Massachusetts aristocrat—who seems such a nice man—with his shoulders slightly slumped and "his modest stomach . . . pushed forward a hint," it occurs to him that

> One did not achieve the languid grandeurs of that slouch in one generation—the grandsons of the first sons had best go through the best troughs in the best eating clubs at Harvard before anyone in the family could try for such elegant note.

Then, as the hours pass with their various preparatory rallies and meetings, the time finally comes for the march and the big push forward across the Potomac to the Pentagon grounds. All the jagged rhythms of the confusion and tension engulfing the great swarming mass of demonstrators are brilliantly rendered, along with the protagonist's fears at once of failing to leave the impress of his own personal spirit on this historic event and of being badly clubbed by the police and the men of the National Guard. Nor does he fail to record his sense of the ambiguity presented by these hordes of young jean-clad protestants against the Vietnam war, for he knows them to be young people believing in "technology" more ardently than any previous generation in history and "gorged on LSD": they, in their own way—their minds "jabbed, poked and twitched" by television—are

> villains . . . now going forth . . . to make war on those other villains, corporation-land villains, who were destroying the promise of the present in their . . . greed and secret lust (often unknown in themselves) for

some . . . variety of neo-fascism. Mailer's final allegiance, however, was to the villains who were hippies.

At last "he was arrested, he had succeeded in that, and without a club on his head . . . he was in the land of the enemy now, he would get to see their face." And so he does, when he confronts the marshals who accompany the arresting MP's—faces "worse then he had expected":

> Some were fat, some were too thin, but nearly all seemed to have those subtle anomalies of the body which come often to men from small towns who have inherited strong features, but end up, by their own measure, in failure. Some would have powerful chests, but abrupt paunches, the skinny ones would have a knob in the shoulder, or a hitch in their gait, their foreheads would have odd cleaving wrinkles, so that one man might look as if an ax had struck him between the eyes, another paid tithe to ten parallel deep lines rising in ridges above his eye brows. The faces of all too many had a low cunning mixed with a stroke of rectitude: if the mouth was slack, the nose was straight and severe; should the lips be tight, the nostrils showed an outside greed. . . . If one could find the irredeemable madness of America . . . it was in those late afternoon race track faces. . . .

In short, Mailer's journalism is marked by the same virtuosity in composition that distinguishes his fiction, by the same incisiveness of portraiture, the same passionate preoccupation with American idiosyncrasy, the same suppleness of syntax and economy of verbal gesture. And it is marked by the same genial malice—as, for example, in his remarking (in *Miami and the Siege of Chicago*) a certain "improvement" in Richard Nixon, the kind of improvement that comes upon a man when he shifts in appearance from looking like an undertaker's assistant to looking like an old con seriously determined to go respectable. The Old Nixon, which is to say the young Nixon, used to look, on clasping his hands in front of him, like a church usher (of the variety who would twist a boy's ear after removing him from church). The older Nixon before the Press now—the *new* Nixon—had finally acquired some of the dignity of the old athlete and the old con—he had taken punishment. . . .

Or, in a similar vein, in his account of the Democratic convention of '68 in Chicago, there is a passage on Hubert Humphrey from which, once it has been read, this gentleman can surely never be rescued. As Mailer recalls how Humphrey looked under the facial cosmetics applied for the television broadcast of his speech in acceptance of the presidential nomination, he says:

Make-up on Hubert's face somehow suggested that the flesh beneath was the color of putty—it gave him the shaky put-together look of a sales manager in a small corporation who takes a drink to get up in the morning, and another drink after he has made his intercom calls: the sort of man who is not proud of drinking; and so in the coffee break, he goes to the john and throws a sen-sen down his throat. All day he exudes odors all over; sen-sen, limewater, pomade, bay rum, deodorant, talcum, garlic, a whiff of the medicinal, the odor of Scotch on a nervous tum, rubbing alcohol!

The voice we hear is of one who intends to defend himself against politicians and against all the official abstractions of a "totalitarian" society, especially when those abstractions are embodied in public men. Which is to say that it is a voice whose intention it is that, amidst a depersonalized and engineered world, some room shall be made (in Yeats's phrase) for "a foolish, passionate man."

Indeed, this foolish, passionate man does not intend to be intimidated even by the flight to the moon. On the contrary, when he flew to Houston and Cape Kennedy in July of 1969 to cover for *Life* Magazine the launching of the flight of Apollo 11, it was with a sense of the event as fraught with unprecedented challenge, but a challenge by which he was not proposing to be overborne. As he says in the huge and brilliantly constructed book which was the result of that mission—*Of a Fire on the Moon* (1970)—he was prepared, yes, to be "a modest quiet observer" in the fantastically technologized world of NASA and the Manned Spacecraft Center just outside of Houston, but he was equally determined that this "spookiest venture in history" should also be at last a genuinely human event and not an occurrence so unreal that it might have been something "staged in a television studio—the greatest con of the century."

The whole atmosphere of the Spacecraft Center is irksome, of course, for a "psychic outlaw": its bleak, windowless, air-conditioned corridors do not make "the coziest home for the human heart." "Aquarius," as he speaks of himself (since he was born under its sign), finds the talk of the astronauts to be, like all bureaucratic talk, an untranslatable jargon "which could be easily converted to computer programming": it is "the anodyne of technologese." Towards these brave and altogether admirable men—Neil Armstrong, Edwin Aldrin, Michael Collins—he wants always to be respectful and courteous, even affectionate; but he cannot refrain from remarking the strange combination they present at once of "banality and apocalyptic dignity." For, though they have "engaged the deepest primitive taboos" and are committed to an odyssey beyond all man's previous journey's-ends, these moonmen from the heartlands of America, with their modest purrs of efficiency and their resolute avoidance of the heroic gesture, are people who on the ground dwell wholly, it seems, amidst the odorless, antiseptic realities of modern technology. They are pushing through toward "that other world where death, metaphysics and the unanswerable questions of eternity must reside"; yet they talk only about "peripheral secondary objectives" and "mobility studies" and integrating "orders of priorities." For they, along with all the space "technologues" on the NASA staff at Houston, are bent on demystifying the world of the interstellar spaces, on making it a new field of engineering, on divesting it of its last element of numinousness. Whereas Mailer wants (in the previously quoted phrase of Richard Foster's) "to steal back, for the languishing forces of 'God,'" what Wordsworth called "the burthen of the mystery," and he wants it to remain the *mysterium tremendum et fascinosum*. Though all the while marvelling at the miracles wrought by the Von Brauns and the Muellers and the Paines and though—simply for the sake of trying to understand their staggering achievements—prepared to become "an acolyte to technology . . . [and] to observe as if he were invisible," he faces the whole enterprise of the National Aeronautics and Space Administration with a certain cranky combativeness and scepticism. Just here, as he makes us feel he supposes, may be the last great blasphemy of our modern technocracy against the holiness of the world, since this voyaging out from Cape Kennedy strikes him as not so much like a valiant attempt at fulfilling the will of God as "like a beast enraged with the passion of gorging nature . . . [wanting] now to make incisions into the platinum satellite of . . . our dreams." And, at the time of the launching, he is struck by the repeated exclamations of an Italian girl with a camera, "*Fenomenal, fenomenal, fenomenal!*"—as he is also struck

by a worker from the MSOB (Manned Spacecraft Operations Building) yelling, "Go get 'em." The moon, in other
words, "was an enemy."

The readers of *An American Dream,* however, will remember Stephen Rojack's dialogues with the moon and
will remember that, for Mailer, the moon is a platinum
lady swathed in a shimmering vestment of silver light who
beckons us toward great risks and high aspirations and who
looks balefully down upon us when the quaverings of fear
hold us back from some hazardous but promising journey
to which we are summoned. Which is to say that, in
Mailer's symbolic universe, the moon is an emblem of
those "unknown modes of being" from whose deeps spring
intimations of eternity. And, though he is fully a man of
the twentieth century who harbors no obscurantist animus
against scientific exploration and who wants to cast no
veto against the astronauts' project, he yet does not want
the moon to be "violated": he wants it, even while it is
being meticulously surveyed, to remain in the world of the
dream. For Mailer, as many of his essays have most insistently averred, is not a Freudian, and dreams are not for
him simply the fulfillments of wishes: instead, they are
"existential" possibilities, they are the ways in which we
plot our human course on this earth. So a flight to the
moon, however properly it may be engineered by the
people of NASA, requires finally to be deemed a property
not of aeronautical science but of the poetic and religious
imagination. Indeed, for all of his frankly acknowledged
lust for riches and glory, *Of a Fire on the Moon* makes us
feel that Mailer went to Texas and to Florida not simply
for the enormous fee that *Life* was prepared to pay a
writer of his celebrity for being on the scene but went,
primarily, to rescue the moon from the "technologues."
His book, therefore, though always carefully deferential
toward Armstrong and Collins and Aldrin and their col-

leagues, is consistently marked by such an archness with
respect to the world of Wernher Von Braun as is prompted
by his determination to preserve a certain threshold of the
numinous which he fears this world is calculated to blot
out. And it is this interest which accounts for his elaborately Yeatsian speculations on the Psychology of Astronauts and the Psychology of Machines, maneuvers that are
only large poetic conceits designed in some partial way to
indemnify our secularized imaginations against NASA's
theft of "magic, psyche, and the spirits of the underworld"
from an extraordinary occasion. The result is a book
whose weight and profundity and charm have been acknowledged only very charily in the critical estimates it
has elicited.

*       *       *

So it is that Norman Mailer has brooded over these past
years on his great subject—which is nothing other than that
"complex fate" which belongs to the American character.
Given the sharply polemical and indictive tenor of his
judgments about the American scene, it might well be felt
to be somewhat astonishing that, since the late sixties, he
has been so widely accorded the kind of approbatory
recognition that he enjoys today, this being made especially notable by a large affectionateness of a sort which no
other American writer of our period commands. Indeed, it
might be felt to be particularly surprising that, for all the
dark and condescending forecasts of his future being made
a decade ago by the "liberal" Establishment, it is now just
from this stronghold that Mailer's most ardent advocates
come. For, like so many of his distinguished predecessors
in modern literary life—like Yeats and Lawrence and Eliot
and Pound—he is a man tenaciously dedicated to ideas and
beliefs many of which are separated from the basic com-

mitments of the liberal, secular mind by a very considerable discrepancy. He sets no great store by urban renewal
and psychoanalysis; he never tires of recording his abhor-
rence of antibiotics and plastics and contraceptives; he
hates that bleak "functionalism" in contemporary architecture and styles of décor created by the epigones of the
Bauhaus; he finds a kind of barbarism represented by the
people who eat scientifically, who copulate scientifically,
who rear their children scientifically. And these familiar
crotchets, in which he is sometimes thought to be too
indulgent, are but an expression of a profound dubiety
about what we are bequeathed, in this late time, by the
Enlightenment—the supposition that the human reality is
to be ordered by the rules of science, that we must live
within the abstractions of the positivist mind, that to rely
on values personally conceived and to trust one's own
experience of the world is to court disaster. The young
couple who buy only what *Consumer Reports* tells them
to buy but who make no purchases at all before consulting
the budget counselor at the neighborhood Co-op Shopping
Center, who do with their child only what is sanctioned by
Dr. Gesell, who decide how to use their franchise only
after getting a set of directives from the League of Inde-
pendent Voters, and who, once they begin to feel like solid
citizens, join the Unitarian Church—these young people, in
their cheerful rationalism, will be regarded by Mailer as
simply victims of the facelessness and "totalitarianism"
that, in his sense of things, now belong to the actual
culture of "liberal democracy." And, as he has maintained
in virtually everything he has written since "The White
Negro," the only effective remedy for the ailments engendered by a totalitarian society is to be found in the realm
not of conventional politics but of a certain kind of
religious radicalism. So he would seem most assuredly to
stand at a great distance from those who represent, politi-

cally and culturally, a left-of-center position; and the endorsement of his career which they are now prepared to give may, therefore, be felt to be indeed something of a puzzle.

This is a puzzle, however, that will appear perhaps to be less perplexing when it is recalled that Mailer's chief stratagem for subverting the totalitarianism of a technocratic culture has entailed his entering into what the English critic Martin Green calls "the Faustian contract." That is to say, instead of entering into the contract that Freud lays down as necessary for the human endeavor in *Civilization and Its Discontents*, instead of exchanging "immediate appetitive gratification for mental and moral pleasures," he has selected another contract which puts, indeed, a high premium on appetite and self-gratification and which involves an exchange of "decorum . . . [and] due proportion . . . for powers of intuitive knowledge"[14] and for a vision of the *Mysterium Tremendum*. It is something like the arrangement chosen by Faust. And, even if this bargain may be viewed with some slight misgivings by the less resilient representatives of the Old Left, it is precisely that aspect of Mailer's affiliations which does manage for the New Left to redeem his secular heterodoxy. For the New Sensibility, in its powerfully antinomian commitment to the preferability of nature over nurture, is persuaded that virtually all collectivities deal aggressively with the self and that, if it is to escape its bondage to this irrational aggressiveness, it must count on a kind of Faustian contract for the attainment of what the cultivated slang of our period denominates as "authenticity." Mailer's conviction, in other words, that no longer is there anything potentially revolutionary in "politics," since it inevitably postulates as

14Martin Green, "Amis and Mailer: The Faustian Contract," *The Month*, 2nd n.s., 3, no. 2 (February, 1971):46.

the normative framework for the human enterprise the old institutional setting which has long since proved to be subversive of authenticity, his conviction that health and blessedness are to be found not in the superego but in the id, that man redeemed is man the "psychic outlaw"—all this is calculated to constitute a very great commendation in his behalf, for a radical mentality which tends now to take an inculpatory view of society as such.

As indentured partly to a Faustian contract, he intends, of course—at least as we are often led to suppose—to be a metaphorist. But his admonitory zeal and his eagerness to alter the course of history are, as we sometimes feel, by way of tempting him to discard his investment in metaphoric modes, in the interests of a more immediately regenerative preachment. And the resulting ambiguity in his thought—"so much moral affirmation coupled with so much moral anarchism"[15] —is precisely of a sort that has frequently appeared supportive of those fashionable contemporary truancies (espoused by such oracles as Norman Brown and R. D. Laing and Herbert Marcuse) that involve some drastic disavowal of the *Polis* as the scene and setting of human existence. His seeming confidence in Whitman's "Nature without check with original energy"; his homeopathic doctrine that "acute disease is cure," that our strength and salubrity are to be found in the madness of the psychic outlaw or philosophical psychopath; his insistence on the necessity of a politics of social reconstruction being superceded by a politics of salvation; his Manichaean vision of God as One needing to be ransomed from the danger He is in of dying; and his great penchant for the apocalyptic gesture—all this does, indeed, seem in some degree to deliver him over to those regions of the New Left

[15]Trilling, "Radical Moralism of Norman Mailer," p. 147.

where the dominant partiality is (in a phrase employed in *The Armies of the Night*) for "revolution by theatre and without a script."

For all of what is profoundly ambiguous and occasionally distressing in Mailer's account of the conditions and procedures of the moral life, it may yet be that we should simply rely upon the prodigiousness of his wit and intelligence to rescue him, finally, from any sort of ethical or political obscurantism with which he may be inclined, once and again, to treat (whether at the level of conceptual hypothesis or of poetic conceit). Irving Howe, to be sure, insists quite properly that

> Mailer as thaumaturgist of orgasm; as metaphysician of the gut; as psychic herb-doctor; as advance man for literary violence; as dialectician of unreason . . . —these masks of brilliant, nutty restlessness . . . —all require sharp analysis and criticism.[16]

But what needs to be kept in mind is that the public roles of this "Nijinsky of ambivalence" (as he calls himself in *Of a Fire on the Moon*) are, indeed, masks; and it is by no means so clear as Mr. Howe supposes that, in the last analysis, they "represent values in deep opposition to liberal humaneness and rational discourse."[17] For, again and again, this extraordinarily brilliant man reveals his capacity to strike through the masks—as, for example, in his uneasy withdrawal in recent years from those young Dantons and Marats who have demetaphorized his metaphors into a program for "revolution by theatre and without a script." It would seem that, after the time of the march on the Pentagon, Mailer increasingly felt ambiguity

[16]Irving Howe, *Decline of the New* (New York: Harcourt, Brace & World, 1970), p. 262.
[17]*Ibid.*, p. 263.

to be mounted on ambiguity—in the hordes of young
desperadoes and true believers assembled under many of
the banners being flourished by the New Left. So by the
summer of 1968, when he moved into Chicago as a report-
er on assignment to cover the national convention of the
Democratic Party, he was beginning to view with more
than a little alarm much of the new radicalism born of the
Vietnam protest movement. During that strange and terrible August week, as he traveled about a city "washed with
the air of battle," he was aghast at the ugly fray finally
arranged by the rioting policemen. But his sense of American society being "held together by bonds no more powerful . . . than spider's silk" was sharpened not only by the
rampant unruliness and criminality of the police, for, as he
faced the thousands of Hippies and Yippies and various
assorted come-outers who had flocked into the city to
badger the political Establishment, he knew that they, too,
represented forces which promised to be powerfully disruptive of the country. Here, to be sure, was a vast com-
pany of young people who were by way of electing to be
psychic outlaws and philosophical psychopaths; yet, when
actually confronted with their hysterical nihilism, Mailer
knew that he did not like it and could not, therefore,
suppress his scepticism about "these odd unkempt children
[being] the sort of troops with whom one wished to enter
battle." He suddenly knew that, for all of its speciousness
and absurdity, "he wanted America to go on—not as it was
going, not Vietnam," but also not up into some apocalyptic blast of holocaust and extinction. And he could not
put aside his realization that the gangs led by Tom Hayden
and Abbie Hoffman could be counted on to do nothing
more than deliver to reactionism "a pretext to bring in
totalitarian phalanxes of law and order." It is, in short, the
honesty with which, in the event, Mailer is to be found to
some extent withdrawing from the creatures of his own

imagination that gives a special significance to his testi-mony in the latter part of *Miami and the Siege of Chicago*.

So he is, indeed, a "Nijinsky of ambivalence" whose future course none can predict with certainty. But of much else we may be certain—namely, that he is today a great primary force in American cultural life; that, what-ever may be the particular projects to which he turns his hand in the coming years, he will continue his brooding on our "complex fate"; and that this extraordinary writer, in his Whitmanesque role as spokesman for the American conscience, will be wanting (with however much idiosyn-crasy) to hold forth a "theory of America" which, in its defense of the "simple separate person," will give voice in a "totalitarian" age to something like the kind of doctrine that Whitman in *Democratic Vistas* called "personalism."

# Bellow's Vision
# of the "Axial Lines"

# III

# Bellow's Vision
# of the "Axial Lines"

In January of 1956, under the auspices of the Gertrude
Clarke Whittall Fund, the late R. P. Blackmur delivered
four lectures at the Library of Congress on the literature of
the nineteen-twenties. As one reads the printed text of
these addresses, it tickles the imagination a little to think
how baffled Blackmur's audience of housewives and students and government clerks must have been by the flail-
ings and thrashings about of the strange kind of language
to which he gave himself in his last years. The little
booklet comprising these lectures which the Library published in 1956[1] affords one of many sad examples of how
great a hardship the attempt at communication had come
to be for this distinguished critic in the late phase of his
career: the addresses are all "great general blobs," such as
Blackmur claimed to find in much of Whitman's poetry,
and an odd sort of vatic delirium in the style makes
everything nearly altogether impenetrable. Yet, here and
there, the darkness is lit up by flashes of the wit and
brilliance of perception that made Blackmur over a long

[1]See R. P. Blackmur, *Anni Mirabiles, 1921-25: Reason in the Madness of Letters* (Washington, D. C.: Reference Department of the
Library of Congress, 1956).

period one of the great princelings of modern criticism: and the first of these is to be found in the very title itself which he gave to these lectures, *Anni Mirabiles,* for this is what he took the early twenties to have been—marvelous years, a time of great harvest in the history of the modern movement. And so indeed the period was: it was a time of glory, a time of wonders, which saw the appearance in 1921 of Pirandello's *Sei personaggi* and some of Pound's most characteristic *Cantos,* in 1922 of Eliot's *The Waste Land* and Joyce's *Ulysses,* in 1923 of Wallace Stevens' *Harmonium* and Rilke's *Duineser Elegien,* in 1924 of Mann's *Der Zauberberg,* in 1925 of Valéry's *M. Teste* and Kafka's *Der Prozess.* And so the decade proceeded, its brilliance being particularly notable on the American scene, where there was a great efflorescence of remarkable creativity: Dreiser's *An American Tragedy* and Fitzgerald's *The Great Gatsby* in 1925, Hemingway's *The Sun Also Rises* in 1926, Wolfe's *Look Homeward, Angel* and Faulkner's *The Sound and the Fury* in 1929. Wonderful years indeed.

Now it has been a habit of American criticism lately to submit the achievement of our writers in this country since the Second World War to various kinds of stock taking and fretfully to speculate on the possibility of regarding the years just gone by as having also been *anni mirabiles.* The twenties and the early thirties are a golden time in American literary life which it is exhilarating to recall. But they are also years that weigh heavily upon us as a challenge, and as a challenge that constantly threatens to become a diminishing reproach if there cannot be descried in our uncertain present the signs of a stature comparable to that splendid insurgency of forty-five years ago. So we are all the time taking polls and making tallies, most especially about our fiction; and when the tabulations prove sometimes to be unfavorable, the resulting dejection turns us suddenly into crestfallen obituarists of the novel. But then new polls will be taken and more tallies made, and the hope will revive of finding the present time to be as fruitful as that of Fitzgerald and Hemingway and Faulkner.

Yet, underneath the fervent encomia that are frequently offered the contemporary scene by the hucksters of *Tendenz*, there is a certain nettling mistrust, and a nagging intuition that, certainly in the novel, the postwar period has not augmented, has not *added* anything to the furniture of the imagination in the way that a truly great literature does. It makes very little sense, however, to launch out into windy pontifications about the death of the novel, for only very rarely does a national literature find writers as gifted as the Fitzgerald of *Gatsby* and the Hemingway of *The Sun Also Rises* and the Faulkner of *The Sound and the Fury* handling the same genre within a single generation. And surely it would be silly to postulate the death of a medium whose most characteristic practitioners today are people so talented as John Barth, Bernard Malamud, William Styron, John Hawkes, Norman Mailer, and Thomas Pynchon. But what counts most heavily against the alarmism of those who pronounce the novel to be dead is the simple fact that, at least on the American scene, we have in Ralph Ellison's novel of 1952, *Invisible Man*, one indubitably great book and that in the fiction of Saul Bellow we have a body of work whose richness in both form and idea promises that his will eventually become one of the great careers in the literary life of the second half of the century.

In Mr. Bellow's case, however—and Mr. Ellison's is not far different—critical assessment frequently has tended to miss its mark to an astonishing extent. When Maxwell Geismar, for example, is not searching out the "psycho-biological [questions] . . . at the base of [his] work," he is undertaking to affiliate Mr. Bellow with "social realism" and proposing that in such a book as *The Victim* he is doing, in terms of lower-middle class Jewish life in New York City, the general sort of thing Orwell was doing in relation to the dinginess of the *petit bourgeois* London world of *Keep the Aspidistra Flying*. Or Mr. Geismar is proposing that such a text as *Seize the Day* presents, in relation to the drab gloom of the upper West Side of New York, essentially the same *kind* of account that a John O'Hara or a John P. Marquand (!) presents in relation to other areas of American life. Mr. Bellow's métier, we are told, is that of "the social realism school of Dreiser . . . and of such later figures as Ira Wolfert, James T. Farrell, and Nelson Algren."[2] It is an amazing verdict, but not unlike that which has been delivered by other critics less committed in principle than Mr. Geismar to the issues of sociology and "psychobiology." A younger and more perceptive man, Marcus Klein, in a book generally marked by a very fine intelligence, has told us, for example, that the problems faced by all of Mr. Bellow's characters "are reducible to a single problem: to meet with a strong sense of self the sacrifice of self demanded by social circumstance."[3] And it is a similar circle of definition that has been flung awkwardly about his work in much of the critical discussion which it has prompted in the last few years.

What is wrong, of course, in this version of things is not that Mr. Bellow's fiction is uninfluenced by any dialectical sense of the individual's relation to society. On the contrary, his books consistently reveal that the question as to

[2]See Maxwell Geismar, "Saul Bellow: Novelist of the Intellectuals," in *American Moderns: From Rebellion to Conformity* (New York: Hill and Wang, 1958), pp. 210-224.

[3]Marcus Klein, *After Alienation: American Novels in Mid-Century* (Cleveland and New York: World Publishing Co., 1964), p. 34.

how the individual needs to respond to the requirements
levied by "social circumstance" is one of his most absorbing preoccupations as a novelist. Yet social circumstance
never defines the ultimate dimension of selfhood in the
world of *Augie March* and *Henderson* and *Herzog:* the
human individual is in no way shown here to be merely an
epiphenomenon of social process: personality is not imagined in ways that suggest it to be wholly immersed in a
social continuum and reaching only towards a social destiny. What is in fact one of the more striking features of
the fiction is that the central moments in the experience of
Mr. Bellow's characters are always, as it were, moments of
*Existenz* in which a man, transcending the immediate
pressures of his environment and the limiting conditions of
the social matrix, asks himself some fundamental question
about the nature of his own humanity. And thus the
contemporary line to which Mr. Bellow belongs is not that
tag end of American naturalists—John O'Hara, Nelson
Algren, Irwin Shaw—who are committed to a dreary autom-
atism of social reportage and who are, to be sure, convinced that there is some "sacrifice of self demanded by
social circumstance." It is, rather, a line reaching from
Penn Warren and Faulkner back toward Mark Twain and
Melville and Hawthorne, and toward the European tradition of Dostoievski and Kafka and Svevo and Sartre—the
line, in other words, of modern fiction whose principal
area of inquiry is the phenomenology of selfhood.

And when, in the particular case of Saul Bellow, I speak
of his novels as entailing an enterprise of phenomenology,
it is not for language then to be too greatly stretched, for
his fiction is in fact, one feels, stirred into life fundamentally by a certain sort of philosophical endeavor.

There comes a time, it will be recalled, in *The Adventures of Augie March* when, after having just barely managed to escape the nets flung at him by all sorts of people

wanting to organize and control his life, Augie finds himself dealing with still another "Machiavellian." Having signed with the Merchant Marine after the outbreak of the War in 1941, he ships out from Boston, two days after his marriage to Stella. But on the fifteenth day out, the *Sam MacManus* is torpedoed, and Augie scrambles into a lifeboat whose other occupant is one Basteshaw, the ship's carpenter, who, with a curious pedantry, holds forth in a high-sounding kind of pompous oratory. As the two drift along over the water together, Basteshaw speaks, for example, of a former girl friend who contracted pulmonary phthisis, a condition which, as he informs Augie "in his lecturer's tone," entails increased temperatures that "often act on the erogenous zones spectacularly." Or, again, this megalomaniac—who has tried all his life "to be as much of a Renaissance cardinal as one can under modern conditions"—undertakes to instruct Augie on what he calls "the reality situation" and describes how his researches in the physiology of boredom eventuated in his learning how to create life, to create protoplasm—some of which had been on the *MacManus*, where he had been continuing his researches. Now that it floats somewhere in the ocean, he contemplates the possibility of his having initiated a new chain of evolution. So it is that this madman's rhetoric moves on to ever greater peaks of extravagance and intensity, till Augie at last thinks weariedly to himself "Why did I always have to fall among theoreticians!" And one cannot help but notice how frequently at other points Mr. Bellow's fiction wants to express a sense of something ambiguously threatening and baleful in the Idea and in those of its servants whose zeal is unqualified and absolute. In his monologue called "Address by Gooley MacDowell to the Hasbeens Club of Chicago,"[4] Gooley speaks of the

[4]Saul Bellow, "Address by Gooley MacDowell to the Hasbeens Club of Chicago," *The Hudson Review*, 4, no. 2 (Summer 1951): 225-26.

"dome of thought" around our heads, "as thick as atmosphere to breathe. . . . One thought leads to another as
breath leads to breath. . . . But a person can no longer keep
up, and plenty are dying of good ideas. We have them in
the millions. . . . What a load you can buy for a buck, in
anthologies, out of Augustine, Pascal, Aristotle, Nicholas
of Cusa, super-brain Goethe. . . . Look at us, deafened,
hampered, obstructed, impeded, impaired and bowel-
glutted with wise counsel and good precept, and the more
plentiful our ideas the worse our headaches. So we ask,
will some good creature pull out the plug and ease our
disgusted hearts a little?" And a similar note is struck in
*Seize the Day* and *Henderson the Rain King* and *Herzog*.

Yet, despite his penchant for viewing with alarm the
brutalizing power of the intellect and the desiccating ef-
fects of modern rationalism, Mr. Bellow is perhaps himself
the outstanding "theoretician" amongst the major novelists of our period, and his books are drenched in specula-
tion. This is not to say that he conceives the novel to be an
essentially expository medium or that he is a "philosophical novelist," in the usual sense of that term, for the
immediate stuff of his art is not an affair of (as Lionel
Trilling would say) those "pellets of intellection" which
are the material of systematic thought: it is, rather, an
affair of enormously larky and vital characters and of the
interesting relationships into which they are brought with
one another and with the world of the American metrop-
olis. But these characters themselves are personages whose
most fundamental interest is a "theoretical" interest, and
therein, Mr. Bellow seems to feel, is the real wellspring of
their humanity.

Joseph, in *Dangling Man*, commits to his journal the
reflection that "We are all drawn toward the same craters
of the spirit—to know what we are and what we are for, to
know our purpose, to seek grace." And this is indeed the
gravitating passion by which Mr. Bellow's people are

moved. Augie March has a great need to ferret out the "axial lines" of life—which is precisely the sovereign aspiration by which Asa Leventhal and Tommy Wilhelm and Eugene Henderson and Moses Herzog are guided. And, as Joseph says, "if the quest is the same, the differences in our personal histories, which hitherto meant so much to us, become of minor importance." So it makes very little difference at what point the reader enters Mr. Bellow's fiction, since wherever he makes his way into it, what he encounters are people like the protagonist of *Seize the Day*—who is, we are told, a "visionary sort of animal. Who has to believe that he can know why he exists." One encounters "theoreticians" whose most passionate commitment is to a very urgent kind of *Lebensphilosophie*, to the kind of vitally *existential* "theorizing" which is a hallmark of many of the central personages in twentieth-century fiction, of Musil's Ulrich and Joyce's Stephen Dedalus, of Lawrence's Birkin and Mann's Hans Castorp, of Malraux's Hernandez and Vincent Berger, of Camus' Rieux and Penn Warren's Jack Burden.

It deserves to be stressed that the inquiry into the meaning of human existence carried forward by Mr. Bellow's protagonists is not, experientially, a bootless thing of abstract dialectic. It is, instead, a search into which they are plunged by the pressure of concrete circumstance, by the wreckage of hope and the bitter taste in their own lives of inauthenticity. One among them tells himself, on a certain crucial day of awakening, that he must undertake a great new effort, that otherwise it is likely that his life will simply wither away, with nothing remaining—"nothing left but junk." And it is indeed the character of rubble, of mess, of disarray, that defines a part of what is initially problematic in the situation of Mr. Bellow's people: they have stumbled into one or another dark and airless pocket of the world—where confidence is broken by piles of little

disappointments, where nerves are rubbed raw by the
cheating and condescension suffered at the hands of du-
plicitous friends and relatives, and where the spirit is
smothered by all the pledges and promises it has made and
found impossible to fulfill. "The world is too much with
us, and there has never been so much world," Mr. Bellow
remarked some years ago in a review of Philip Roth's
*Good-bye, Columbus*; and this is very much the sort of
complaint one imagines his own characters wanting weariedly to express as they face the human bustle and density
of their drab little space amidst the great noisy, sprawling
urban wilderness—which, whether it is encountered in Chicago by an Augie March or in New York by a Tommy
Wilhelm, requires to be thought of as a "somber city."
"Hot, stony odors" rise up from subways, and traffic
seems to "come down . . . out of the sky": everything is
draped with soot, and nowhere does one hear any happy
"epithalamium of gentle lovers." The scene or site of the
novels is—as in Joyce's *Ulysses*, in Canetti's *Auto da Fé*, in
Dos Passos's *The Big Money*, in Graham Greene's *It's a
Battlefield*—"a populous and smoky city," where one
would not have thought "death had undone so many."

The stars are capricious, and the burdens that people
must bear exact, therefore, a great expense of spirit. As a
consequence, their fingernails are bitten and their eyes
red-rimmed, and they often do not feel well, suffering a
sense of "congestion" or extremes of fatigue, an obscure
pain in the side or a raging headache—signs that they have
not done well in their isolation. Joseph, the young man
whose diary (composed in the months during which he
awaits his call-up into the army) forms Mr. Bellow's first
book—the novel of 1944, *Dangling Man*—no longer takes
any real delight in his devoted wife Iva. He explodes at the
members of his family and picks quarrels with his friends,
"storing bitterness and spite which eat like acids at [his]

endowment of generosity and good will." Gripped by a strange "narcotic dullness," he is growing fat and slovenly, as more and more—like Beckett's Murphy—he becomes "rooted to [his] chair." Or, again, Asa Leventhal, the unheroic hero of Mr. Bellow's second novel, *The Victim* (1947), has slipped into early middle age as one who has just barely missed failure in the world of the city's job market: he edits a small New York trade paper, but his competence at the job does not altogether allay his intermittent anxiousness about the security of his tenure. He is attentive to his brother's wife and children in the brother's absence, but grudgingly so. Like the young protagonist of *Dangling Man*, he turns a dour peevishness and spleen upon his friends and is given to nursing imagined slights and insults. He often does not even bother to answer the friendly greeting of a waitress in a restaurant, though he tells himself that he ought to be more responsive. His burly, disheveled figure presents an appearance which is "unaccommodating, impassive," and, in the oppressive heat of a New York summer, he sweats profusely and suffers headache and heart tremor and a sense of his very head being filled with the pungent odors of the city. But even more blistered by experience is Tommy Wilhelm, the protagonist of the brilliant *novella* of 1956, *Seize the Day*—a man without work and very nearly penniless; badgered for money by the wife from whom he is separated and scorned by his smug, unfeeling father; ruined in physique and going to seed in every way, yet desperately scrounging about New York for some merest foothold—a man whose throat is nearly bursting with a "great knot of ill and grief" as his "day of reckoning" approaches. And that great Tarzan of a man whom we meet in *Henderson the Rain King* (1959), for all of his millions and for all of his rude health and energy, knows how onerous it is to "lie buried in yourself" and be filled with an aching need to

"burst the spirit's sleep." Indeed, not even the irrepressible
little *picaro* of *The Adventures of Augie March* (1953) is
untouched by the generalized *malaise* of Mr. Bellow's
world, for at every turn he finds himself surrounded by
"destiny moulders . . . and wizard evildoers, bigwheels and
imposers-upon." And the city against the background of
which most of his drama is played out is a place of crime
and violence and suffering. The world that this fiction
takes us into is of a sort to put us in mind of the old
monition, "Though he believe it, no man is strong."

Yet the effect of these books is never depressive and
enervating, and their personae are not felt, in the end, to
be denizens of the Underground: indeed, I first spoke of
their great vitality and—using a piece of Mr. Bellow's
favorite slang—of their "larkiness": and this, curiously, is
the final impression they make upon us, of being, most of
them, very larky people. The sense of animation and
exuberance that we are given comes in part from the
buoyant language of which Mr. Bellow is so brilliantly
vivacious an impresario. In many of the marvelously subtle
and perspicacious essays making up his book of 1962, *The
Barbarian Within*, Fr. Walter Ong is reminding us of a
truism frequently forgotten by a generation whose most
characteristic mentors in criticism have taught us to believe
"that it is neither the potter who made it nor the people,
real or fictional, to whose lives it is tangent, but the well
wrought urn itself which counts. . . ."[5] The great preoccupation of contemporary criticism has been with *the text*,
with the work of art *as such*, for it has been supposed that
only by squinting at the poem or the novel as an *object*
can criticism so locate norms by which its discourse may
become really corrigible. But, this line of thought having

[5]Walter J. Ong, S.J., *The Barbarian Within* (New York: Macmillan
Co., 1962), p. 15.

long since been driven more than ragged, it is good that such a theorist as Fr. Ong should now remind us again of what ought never to have been forgotten, that a work of literary art, in its most primitive reality, is something "said"—not simply an object clearly and distinctly framed in space, but a "word" spoken *by one man*, "a moment in a dialogue."[6] The "voice" of the artist is conveyed, of course—as Fr. Ong fully understands—through the "objective" structures of poetry and fiction and drama: which is to say that its invocations and evocations are accomplished through the artist's various "masks." But the writer's mask is not itself vocal: it is an instrument (whether of plot or scene or "point of view") whereby the voice is enabled to register interesting variations in tone and pitch and rhythm and stress, but it does not itself modify the authorial voice in the way that a mute modifies the sound of a violin.[7] So, given the primitively vocal and aural character of literary experience, it is the *voice* which is heard in a work of art that remains one of the principal realities inviting the disciplined attention of that uncommon reader whom Virginia Woolf generously called "the common reader." And it is, I want now to say, the voice that one constantly hears, and overhears, in Mr. Bellow's fiction which does in part give us so great a sense of the lively suppleness of the human reality being portrayed.

Here, for example, are the opening lines of *The Adventures of Augie March:*

> I am an American, Chicago born . . . and go at things as I have taught myself, free-style, and will make the record in my own way: first to knock, first admitted; sometimes an innocent knock, sometimes a not so inno-

[6]*Ibid.*, p. 36.

[7]The analogy is Fr. Ong's, though his use of it differs somewhat from mine: *ibid.*, p. 60.

cent. But a man's character is his fate, says Heraclitus, and in the end there isn't any way to disguise the nature of the knocks by acoustical work on the door or gloving the knuckles.

These sentences, in their cascading bounce and friskiness and wit, could by no stretch of the imagination be thought to have come from the pen of a Hemingway or a Faulkner or a Penn Warren, or indeed from that of anyone other than Saul Bellow: the voice (though "masked" by the persona of the novel's hero) is unmistakably his—a voice that says in effect, "Gee, what a funny, mysterious, surprising bloke man is, even when he's on his uppers! What shrewdness it takes to keep up with his craft and enterprise! How inspiriting it is to think that, maybe, things finally will give way—before intelligence and good humor and *esprit*. But how necessary it is that we not tell ourselves lies and that we not lose our sense of how wonderful is the gift of life!" This is the voice that one hears throughout these books, even when it is speaking of suffering and humiliation and despair; and it is this voice that makes even an Asa Leventhal or a Tommy Wilhelm somehow larky.

But what is most decisive in the shaping of character in Mr. Bellow's fiction is the resoluteness with which he refuses to allow his people merely to wriggle in their despondency and dispeace. The texture of their lives is banal and gritty, because, one imagines, this is what Mr. Bellow takes to be the general quality of life in our great metropolitan communities, and his people do therefore bear upon themselves the characteristic stigmata of the age—its *anomie*, its nostalgia, its alienation. But he will not permit them to rest in their distress: they carry great burdens, but Mr. Bellow's way of plotting the human story requires that they be brought to the point of attempting *dis*burdenment: though they are nagged by the "feeling of alienation," a way is prepared by which they may come to understand, as the young protagonist of *Dangling Man* says, that "we should not make a doctrine of our feeling." So the old journalist Schlossberg, in *The Victim*, says, "Choose dignity." And there comes a time when Henderson feels called upon to say sternly to himself: "Henderson, put forth effort." And Moses Herzog, for all of his "schooling in grief" and weighed down as he is by trouble, is finally brought, like Asa Leventhal, to "a kind of recognition," that he owes the powers that created him "a human life." And it is a similar *anagnorisis* towards which the human drama tends generally to move throughout Mr. Bellow's work.

This drama becomes explicitly a drama of reconciliation, however, only in the late books, in *Seize the Day* and *Henderson the Rain King*, in *Herzog* and *Mr. Sammler's Planet:* in the early books grace is more a hope than a reality. And it is in *Dangling Man* that we get the most tenuous and the most muted expression of this hope. Here, the central figure is Joseph, a young "apprentice in suffering and humiliation," who at the outbreak of the Second World War gives up his job in a Chicago travel bureau to await his draft-call. And, in the months that follow, he retires to the little cell that he and his wife occupy in a rooming house, there to become an "earnest huntsman of himself," as he anticipates "the minor crises of the day" (". . . the maid's knock, the appearance of the postman, programs on the radio. . .") and contemplates what may be involved in the vocation of a good man. But he soon falters in his "retreat," and, far from becoming a happy experience of deepened self-recognition, it does instead prove to be a sterile *cul-de-sac* in which Joseph finds himself increasingly defenseless before a strangely disabling inertia that settles down upon him. His predicament begins, paradoxically, to be that of a man *trapped* in his freedom. And he is quite free: Iva, his wife, earns their living: so he is free of any formal daily appointments: and, keeping his distance from friends and family (except for an occasional encounter), he is free of virtually all human involvements. But his solitude is not a rich and fecund thing, but arid and debilitating. As he admits in his diary, "I have begun to notice that the more active the rest of the world becomes, the more slowly I move. . . . I grow rooted to my chair." And though, as he says, "I am unwilling to admit that I do not know how to use my freedom," nevertheless, day after day as he sits in his room, rooted to his chair and anticipating the minor crises of the day, his freedom becomes a cheerless void—in which this descendant of Dostoievski's Underground Man and Goncharov's Oblomov and Svevo's Zeno simply dangles. He is jailed in the prison of his own ego, and, thus doubled back upon himself, it is no wonder that "bitterness and spite" corrode his "endowment of generosity and good will." He thinks that the end of all our striving, the goal towards which man perennially has to struggle, is "pure freedom." But, at last, soured as his life is in the acedia of its isolation, he cannot put aside the realization that, if indeed it is freedom which is the proper goal of man, this must surely be a freedom *from* precisely that into which he has too deeply entered—namely, one's own private selfhood. The self needs somehow to escape its own cage, to avoid being "humped protectively" over its own life. He is forced, in short, to admit: "I had not done well alone." And thus, in its stress on the need for self-transcendence, the book takes a step toward what were to be the principal emphases of Mr. Bellow's later fiction. But it is only the merest step, for Joseph's illumination issues in nothing more than a hastily written note to his Draft Board requesting that he be called up "at the earliest possible moment." And on his last civilian day, as Iva is packing his things, he inwardly exults at being now "in other hands": "Hurray for regular hours! And for the supervision of the spirit! Long live regimentation!" But not even the manifest irony with which these final lines are carefully fringed can quite obscure the paltriness of the Army as a redemptive principle, in the kind of spiritual context which Mr. Bellow's narrative so brilliantly establishes. So his book of 1944 strikes us as making a testimony which is, finally, too provisional, and as thus lacking an ultimate cogency. But in the degree to which it finds its center in a "theoretician" whose great hope is for a new "colony of the spirit," it can now be seen to have been presaging the main course of Mr. Bellow's later fiction.

His second novel, *The Victim* (1947), is no less provisional and indecisive, in its embrace of a cathartic principle, than *Dangling Man*. But Mr. Bellow here implicates his protagonist, Asa Leventhal—like Joseph, a "theoretician" who hovers over "craters of the spirit"—in a complex structure of human actions and relationships which requires him to do something more than merely engage in continuous self-interrogation. But he is by no means exempted from the embarrassments of self-arraignment. For one hot summer evening, in the little neighborhood park near his New York apartment building, he is suddenly approached by a shabby bystander whom, with some exertion of memory, he recognizes as a man he had known very slightly a few years earlier, Kirby Allbee. Allbee was then working on the staff of a trade magazine and had arranged for Leventhal, who was unemployed at the time, to be interviewed by his editor. The interview went badly, with Asa responding irately to the provocative boorishness of Rudiger, and the anger of these exchanges did in fact lead the editor not only to throw Leventhal out of his office but even to fire Allbee for having proposed the meeting. And now Allbee, meeting Leventhal for the first time in several years, accuses him of being the real cause not only of his dismissal from *Dill's Weekly* but also of his subsequent decline, irreversibly, into failure and hand-to-mouth impoverishment. Indeed, Allbee charges Leventhal—to Asa's utter astonishment—with having deliberately undertaken, on the day of that interview, to ruin him, in retaliation for some outburst of anti-Semitism that he had delivered himself of at a party a few nights earlier and that he knows Leventhal to have overheard. It is a strange indictment in response to which Leventhal can only sputter confusedly: "I haven't thought about you in years, frankly. . . . What, are we related?" And, laughing surlily, Allbee answers: "By blood? No, no . . . heavens!"

But how then are they related? This is the issue the novel wants to explore. Here is a New York Jew—an obscure functionary in the great machine of the city's business—living a careful, conventional, apparently irreproachable life. And then, all of a sudden—like the abrupt appearance of Joseph K.'s accuser at the beginning of Kafka's *Der Prozess*—a paranoiac anti-Semite accosts him and bitterly complains of the injury he has suffered at Leventhal's hands. Nor do matters end there. For in his wife's absence—Mary is helping her recently widowed mother move from Baltimore to Charleston—his self-declared victim, claiming no longer to have shelter, invades his flat, soiling it with his personal filth, upsetting the normal routines of Leventhal's tidy life, secretly ransacking personal papers to take possession even of the intimacies of Asa's marriage, and finally taking over his very bed to couple with a woman he brings in from the streets. And, strangely, Leventhal acquiesces in all this outrageous plunderage. For the force of Allbee's reiterated accusations unsettles him to the point of compelling him to look back into the past. And as he inquires into his own motives and solicits the judgments of friends who were privy to the circumstances of a few years ago which Allbee has now called up, he does indeed begin to feel that perhaps this man is not, as he first claims, solely responsible for his own misfortune, that perhaps he, Asa, has himself in some measure contributed to it. This uncouth paranoiac is not wholly right in all his furious allegations, but then he may not be wholly wrong—and, once he begins inwardly to make this admission, Leventhal's defenses against his adversary are effectively broken, and he is entrained towards discovering the true meaning of his own humanity.

In what ways are we really members one of another? If we shoot a bird, do we wound ourselves? How is a man related to his neighbor? What is the full meaning of responsibility? These are the questions that bristle before this perplexed defendant. At first he wants simply to say: "Why pick on me? I didn't set this up any more than you did. Admittedly there was a wrong, a general wrong." But Allbee will not let him off the hook and persists in saying *You! . . . You! . . . You!*

One Sunday afternoon, as Leventhal sits in a restaurant with a group of friends, he listens to the wise old journalist, Schlossberg, reflecting on the difficult equilibrium that man's nature requires him to seek: "It's bad to be less than human and it's bad to more than human." And there comes a time when Leventhal's conscience begins to enforce upon him the hard truth that to be "human" is indeed to be "accountable in spite of many weaknesses," is to be in fact one's brother's keeper. But is there, then, a point beyond which the keeping of one's brother becomes "more than human"? So it would seem. For on a certain night Leventhal wakens to find gas pouring out of his kitchen oven: in an attempt at suicide Allbee would have murdered him as well. So he throws him out: further to temporize with this unhappy creature would be both more *and* less than human.

Then, a few years later, Leventhal (now solidly successful) and his wife are in a theatre one evening where, after the second curtain, by chance they meet Allbee in the lobby. This final episode is curiously tentative and indistinct. Though Allbee, having apparently made some sort of recovery, is elegantly dressed and squiring about a once famous actress, Leventhal, as he faces him, is given a sense of decay. And though Allbee, as he recalls that earlier period in his life, faces Leventhal shamefacedly and with self-mockery, he yet manages to say, as he presses Asa's hand, "I know I owe you something." And so he does, but each is in the other's debt. For it was through Allbee's demoniac agency that Leventhal was brought to a "kind of recognition"—that we cannot choose whom to love, that we are required to love all homeless men who require to be sheltered under our care, lest (as Auden says)

> . . . we make a scarecrow of the day,
> Loose ends and jumble of our common world,
> And stuff and nonsense of our own free will. . . .

So the initial phase of Mr. Bellow's fiction may be considered to form a movement from the stiflingly solipsistic atmosphere of a first novel, marked by all the modish isolationism of the modern *avant-garde*, towards a substantially greater positivity of affirmation—that "No man is an Iland, intire of it selfe. . . ."

Thus the way had already been prepared for the magnificent book which he published in 1953, *The Adventures of Augie March*. In his *New Republic* review of *Augie*, Robert Penn Warren remarked the extent to which Mr. Bellow's essay in "the apparent formlessness of the autobiographical-picaresque novel" in the book of 1953 represented a radical departure from "the Flaubert-James tradition" which he had turned to such brilliant account in his first two novels. And this turning did undoubtedly, at the time, give the public an astonished sense of a certain melodramatism in Mr. Bellow's career as a writer, for the tightness of structure and mutedness of style characteristic of his early work seemed in no way to have presaged the pyrotechnical extravagance of language and narrative procedure marking *The Adventures of Augie March:* in 1953, it appeared to be the most surprising development in the literary life of the period. But, startling as the changes were that Mr. Bellow was negotiating in the basic style of his artistry, it may be that they would not have been quite so startling had *The Victim* been read more closely, for the moral meaning of that book might well have been taken, logically, to entail an inevitable turning towards a more open form.

Unlike the Joseph of *Dangling Man,* who is drawn into himself and who, as a consequence, is hard and inflexible, Augie is a tractable and resilient young man endowed not with "singleness of purpose" but with an unquenchable hospitality toward experience. And thus he "circles"—uncommittedly, and believing that "gods [may] turn up anywhere"—from managing a sporting-goods shop in Evanston to training an eagle for iguana hunting in Mexico, from running a Chicago coal yard to consorting with Trotsky's lieutenants in Mexico City, from vagabondage in Detroit to black-market operations in Paris, from Depression poverty to post-World War II affluence. He is an ebullient *picaro* in search of a fate he can regard as worthy of his natural endowments, and it is his insatiable appetite for adventure that gives the novel its huge expansiveness, causing it to span continents and generations and to make room for nearly a hundred personages, altogether remarkable in their vital eccentricity and vividness of presence. Many years ago, in discussing Theodore Dreiser, Mr. Bellow expressed admiration for Dreiser's great "lifting power," for his ability to make his fiction "lift up" great masses of human actuality, of American experience, of social fact. And it is a similar "lifting power" that helps to make *The Adventures of Augie March* so impressive a feat of the novelistic imagination: it notices and names and evokes and gathers in so rich an abundance of material that its teeming world seems barely once removed from the existential reality of the modern world itself. Mr. Bellow says: "The great pleasure of the book was that it came easily. All I had to do was be there with buckets to catch it." And this is indeed the impression that the novel makes upon us—this sense of a beautifully easy improvisation being, however (as Penn Warren reminded us in his review of the book), "a dramatic illusion . . . [which is] the last sophistication of the writer. . . ."

But though Augie never finds that which he can confidently accept as "a worthwhile fate," he keeps the "opposition" that old Einhorn in Chicago discovered in him as a boy. And, for all of the pliancy which permits him to play the games of so many different people (the young bookthief, Padilla; the trade unionist, Grammick; the unbalanced millionaire and researchist on the "history of human happiness," Robey; the Trotskyite Frazer; the Armenian lawyer and black-marketeer, Mintouchian), there comes a point when he must always "offer resistance and . . . say 'No!'" to those who want to manage and manipulate his life—whether it be to his brother Simon, who wants him to make money and become a big wheel; or to the Renlings, who want him to be their adopted son and heir; or to Thea Fenchel, who asks a self-dedication to her special sort of underworld; or to the various others under whose influence he is brought by the adventures of life. Thus the persistent rhythm of the book is (as the English critic Tony Tanner has astutely observed) "a drifting into things finally stopped by a sudden digging in of the heels or a sudden flight from attachment," [8] for Augie

[8]Tony Tanner, *Saul Bellow* (Edinburgh: Oliver and Boyd, 1965), p. 48.

does not want, as he says, to be "sucked into ... [any] of those ... currents where I can't be myself." It is as Einhorn says: "You've got *opposition* in you. You don't slide through everything. You just make it look so." Clem Tambow tells Augie that he "can't adjust to the reality situation," and to this he is not inclined to offer any rebuttal, for he knows himself to be one who wants "to have a charge counter to the central magnetic one and dance his own dance on the periphery."

So Augie always has "trouble being still" and never has "any place of rest"—and this is why, I suspect, the novel over which he presides lacks any true conclusion. Yet this young "American, Chicago born," wants always very much to find a way of being still, since his great hope, he says, "is based upon getting to be still so that the axial lines can be found." This, to be sure, is his most basic passion (as it is of all those "theoreticians" whom Mr. Bellow elects to a pivotal position in his books), finding the "axial lines" of life. But though, by the end, there is no evidence of Augie's having ever really found this lambent center of gravity, he persists, nevertheless, in his refusal to "live a disappointed life." As he says on the final page of the novel, with his characteristic insouciance, "I may well be a flop at this line of endeavor. Columbus too thought he was a flop, probably, when they sent him back in chains. Which didn't prove there was no America." Yet, finally, Augie has at least won through to the crucial insight that leads directly into the remarkable novels of Mr. Bellow's maturity—that, as he says, "When striving stops, there they are [the "axial lines"] as a gift."

Now it is just here that we are brought to what indeed seems the axial line of Mr. Bellow's whole vision of the world, most particularly as it is expressed in the late books, in *Seize the Day* (1956) and *Henderson the Rain King* (1959) and *Herzog* (1965)—that when striving stops, there it is, the infinitely poignant fullness and beauty of the very miracle of life itself. What we confront, in other words, in this whole body of fiction is a radically religious perspective on the human reality. For though Mr. Bellow's protagonist is characteristically, like Joseph in *Dangling Man*, a "creature of plans" and projects, the recognition that he has ultimately to achieve, particularly in the late novels, is that his plans and projects must at last yield before those tidal rhythms of life which ordain (as it is put in one of the Anglican Prayerbook's most famous Collects) that "in returning and rest we shall be saved, in quietness and in confidence shall be our strength," and that we shall be brought by the Spirit to that Presence "where we may be still. . . ."

"Damn braces, bless relaxes," says a wise half-truth of William Blake's ("half," because, in certain areas of experience, it may be equally important to make the converse testimony). And it is a similar thing that Saul Bellow is often wanting also to say, that there is a certain ultimate dimension in the life of the human spirit in which strenuousness is of no real avail; that true sanity of mind and heart is not won by grabbing at life, by jamming our barns full and packing our banks tight[9]; that moving about the world "with clenched fists even though we keep them in our pockets"[10] does not lead to abundance of life; that *fullness* of life cannot be accumulated "like bank notes or garments"[11]; that the kleptomania which prompts us to

[9]See Samuel H. Miller, *The Great Realities* (New York: Harper & Bros., 1955), p. 162. The quotations from this book which are cited in the four footnotes immediately following acknowledge my indebtedness to the language of one of the most beautifully written and brilliantly original essays in ascetical theology of our time.

[10]*Ibid.*, p. 160.

[11]*Ibid.*, p. 164.

fill "our little backyards with all kinds of things"[12] which strenuousness can lay hands on only makes our last state worse than the first; and that, therefore, we must not "force the saw, flail the wind, beat the waves, uproot the seed"[13]: for, when striving stops, there it all is, as a gift—of Grace.

In my citation of the Anglican Collect for Quiet Confidence, I will perhaps appear to be wanting to bring the design of Mr. Bellow's thought into the *ambiance* of things that are distinctively Christian. But to attempt this would surely be an error in tact and in definition, for the ethos of his fiction is, of course, manifestly drenched in the life and lore of Jewish experience. And one suspects, indeed, that Mr. Bellow's great sympathy for something like a doctrine of *sola gratia* is a consequence of his having been influenced, at some very deep level of his mind and sensibility, by the Hasidic strain of Jewish spirituality. But the essential thrust that I am here remarking need not be given any "denominational" tag at all. For it can be taken to be a "natural law" governing the life-world of the *homo religiosus*, that (as Simone Weil phrased it) "by pulling at the bunch, we make all the grapes fall to the ground,"[14] and that the way into Truth and Felicity is therefore (to change the metaphor) the way of "letting oneself fall"— like "the first flight of a baby eagle, pushed out of the nest by its parents, and then discovering to its amazement that the invisible ocean of light in which it is dropping is capable of bearing it up."[15] In the life that is lived at the

---

[12]*Ibid.*, p. 162.

[13]*Ibid.*, pp. 164-165.

[14]Simone Weil, *Gravity and Grace*, trans. Arthur Wills (New York: G. P. Putnam's Sons, 1952), p. 171.

[15]Karl Heim, *The Transformation of the Scientific World View* (London: S.C.M. Press, 1951), p. 167.

Center of life there is no straining, no muscular effort, but
only a certain kind of strict attentiveness and (as Gabriel
Marcel terms it) *invocation*. There, at the Center, we
consent to take our hands off our lives and simply to
wait—for the stroke of Grace: it is something like this that
is said in the *Bhagavad-Gita* and by Lao-Tse, in the Hasid-
ism of the Baal-Shem-Tov and by Meister Eckhart. "Damn
braces, bless relaxes." And it is also a kind of *falling*-into
Peace which seems to be the essential reality being dramatized in the late work of Saul Bellow.

It is perhaps in *Henderson the Rain King* that this
salient principle of Mr. Bellow's fiction finds its clearest
rendering, though it is their inattentiveness to its presence
in *Seize the Day* which has, I suspect, led many of his
critics to be so baffled, finally, by that brilliant *novella*.
Mr. Bellow tells us that "shoulders are from God and
burdens too," and the harried protagonist of *Seize the
Day*, Tommy Wilhelm, seems to have received more than
his share of God's largesse. This ex-actor and ex-salesman is
unemployed and, having fallen behind in the world's rat
race, at forty-seven years of age is without any hopeful
prospect at all: he is down to his last seven hundred
dollars, and the wife from whom he is separated is brutally
pressing in her insistence upon absolute promptness in his
rendering of the support payments. Nor will the cold little
philistine who is his father—a formerly distinguished physi-
cian now living in comfortable retirement—assist him in
any way at all, not even with the cheap help of words of
encouragement. And, in addition to all the external disarray in Tommy's life, he is himself, despite desperate
attempts to keep up appearances, fast going to seed, his
body spoiled with fat and broken-windedness, with neurotic over-eating and phenobarbital.

Indeed, the day recorded in Mr. Bellow's narrative is the
"day of reckoning" that has rapidly been drawing near: "a

huge trouble long presaged but till now formless was due."
"I'm so choked up and congested . . . I can't see straight,"
Tommy moans, as he contemplates the wreckage of his
foundered life and grows terrified by the thought that he
may even have thrown away his last seven hundred dollars
in permitting the self-declared psychologist, Dr. Tamkin,
to manage it in stock market speculations. Nor does this
surmise prove to be amiss, for, when he goes in search of
the wily little confidence man ("full of high sentence"
about "seizing the day"), he finds that he has absconded.
And it is as he is chasing Tamkin along Broadway on a hot,
bright afternoon that he finds himself suddenly shoved by
the crowds into a funeral parlor where a ceremony happens just then to be in progress. As he looks down at the
dead man, Tommy's "eyes shone hugely with instant
tears," and, "standing a little apart," he begins to weep.

He cried at first softly and from sentiment, but soon
from deeper feeling. He sobbed loudly and his face grew
distorted and hot, and the tears stung his skin. . . .
  Soon he was past words, past reason, coherence. He
could not stop. The source of all tears had suddenly
sprung open within him, black, deep, and hot, and they
were pouring out and convulsed his body, bending his
stubborn head, bowing his shoulders, twisting his face,
crippling the very hands with which he held the hand-
kerchief. His efforts to collect himself were useless. The
great knot of ill and grief in his throat swelled upward
and he gave in utterly and held his face and wept. He
cried with all his heart. . . .
  The flowers and lights fused ecstatically in Wilhelm's
blind, wet eyes; the heavy sea-like music came up to his
ears. It poured into him where he had hidden himself in
the center of a crowd by the great and happy oblivion
of tears. He heard it and sank deeper than sorrow,

through torn sobs and cries toward the consummation of his heart's ultimate need.

One feels that these concluding lines of the story might well have been given such a postscript as T. S. Eliot's "Shantih shantih shantih," for, as they speak of "the consummation of his heart's ultimate need," they announce this unhappy man's having finally been touched by a "Peace which passeth understanding." But though this peace surpasses the understanding in precisely the way of all miracles of Grace, it ought not, *in this way*, to have surpassed, as it has, the understanding of so many of Mr. Bellow's critics who have fidgeted over what they have taken to be its gratuitousness and have sometimes, in exasperation, simply dismissed it out of hand, finally, as an illicit *tour de force*. For the point is—the *dramatic* point is—that, in the hour of his great extremity, Tommy Wilhelm, by the sheer force of his heart's pain, is disarmed into taking his hands off his life, into giving up his struggle, into surrendering, simply surrendering, to the mystery of his own existence. And, when striving stops, there it is—the consummation of his heart's ultimate need and a strange new kind of peace, inevitably at first inchoate and indistinct, but which promises that he may yet survive his distress: he is by way, willy nilly, of *falling* into blessedness.

It is, essentially, the same sort of adventure in atonement which is dramatized in *Henderson the Rain King*. When the book appeared in 1959, it was somehow well received despite the confusion with which many of Mr. Bellow's critics rubbed their eyes and wondered what it is *really* about. But if his commitment to the principle of *sola gratia* be remembered, the novel should present no great puzzle. Its hero, Eugene Henderson—Mr. Bellow's only Gentile protagonist—is a titan of a man whose fortune runs into millions and whose life is cluttered not only with money but with wives and children and mistresses and estates and servants. Yet he suffers a great sense of insufficiency: there is a voice within him constantly crying, "I want, I want, I want," and he feels a nagging compulsion to "burst the spirit's sleep." So he goes off to Africa, "the ancient bed of mankind," in quest of a Great Awakening. And, there, his tutelage falls into the hands of two tribes, the Arnewi and the Wariri.

The Arnewi are a benign, easy going, placid people whose quiet life is badly ruffled by the strenuous dynamism of this chaotic Yankee. They are cattle raisers, but they do not eat beef, for they regard their cattle as their relatives, not as domestic animals. At the time Henderson enters their village the people are stricken with grief, for, not being able to water their cattle, the cows are rapidly dying of thirst—and the cattle cannot be watered because a great batch of frogs has gotten into the village cistern, and the people are prevented by religious scruples from removing the frogs, though they believe the frogs to be contaminating the water: they think they are suffering a plague sent by the gods. So Henderson determines to come to their assistance—but, in attempting to explode the frogs out of the water, he blows up the cistern as well. And, having visited this disaster upon the Arnewi, he must then, of course, leave. But, before his short stay amongst them is over, he has an interview with Willatale, the old lady who with an impressive dignity presides over these people as their Queen. This interview brings him great solace, because of what he feels to be the sensitive penetration with which the Queen perceives his heart's deepest aspiration, when she says to him, "Grun-tu-molani"—which means "Man want to live."

Henderson's most crucial encounter, though, is with the Wariri—who are, as his guide Romilayu tells him, "chillen dahkness." And indeed their rites and manners are cruder, very much more savage and violent, than those of the Arnewi. But their King, Dahfu, is a man of great gentleness and sophistication who makes Henderson feel immediately "that we could approach ultimates together." And so they do. For, after Henderson survives certain initial tests, Dahfu with great patience undertakes his education in the things of the spirit. "Granted, grun-tu-molani is much," says Dahfu, "but it is not alone sufficient. Mr. Henderson, more is required." So he prescribes a most exigent discipline. It involves a daily descent into the den of a lion which Dahfu has himself trapped and tamed and which he keeps in an underground vault beneath his palace. Henderson is "all limitation . . . contracted and cramped"—"self-recoiled"—and Dahfu perceives that this man who all his life has inwardly cried, "I want, I want, I want," must be taught how to relax. And his way of doing this involves his requiring Henderson each day to draw nearer and nearer to the lion, and finally to romp about the den on all fours, roaring and snarling as loudly as his lungs will permit.

Thus it is that Dahfu takes Henderson to "the bottom of things," being certain that if his American visitor can learn, like the lion, "not [to] take issue with the inherent" and to relax, his fear will be overcome and his "consciousness [will be made] to shine": his excessive "ego-emphasis" will be mitigated, will be "loosened up." Then he can move into the profound peace that comes when a man is no longer glued to his own finitude but when, having learned to submit to Being itself, he can be claimed by a waft of Grace and delivered into perfect felicity. "Damn braces, bless relaxes": this is what Dahfu wants to say to his pupil. And, indeed, Henderson's last state is better than the first, for the importunate voice within—"I want, I want, I want"—has been stilled. At the end, when the plane on which he is bound for New York stops at Newfoundland for fuel and he gets out to leap about "over the pure white lining of the gray Arctic silence," he is a man whose spirit's sleep has been pierced. No longer does he need to *rush* through the world in the old way, for he has broken out of the cycle of *becoming* and into the realm of *being*—because, back there, with Dahfu he became (in Rilke's phrase) a "deeply kneeling man."

Here, of course, one feels that Mr. Bellow's eagerness to enunciate a principle of redemption released an allegorical passion so rampant as to have very nearly overwhelmed altogether his commitment to the novel as a form. In retrospect, it seems that the exuberant sportiveness of the language in which the book is written and the rich inventiveness with which scene and incident are created may have produced the illusion of novelistic structures which in fact have been virtually suspended. Yet, if Henderson—with his size-22 collar and his enormous bulk and his aching teeth and his pig farm and his two wives and all his millions—is more a presence than a man, he is certainly the most memorable comic presence in recent fiction. And though his outrageous shenanigans and buffoonery sometimes come close to parodying Mr. Bellow's deeper meanings, this writer's *deepest* meaning may well be that the kind of nonchalance about itself which is expressed in self-parody can easily be afforded by a humanity whose "ego-emphasis" has been "loosened up" by the realization that the gift of life is to be had only "when striving stops."

Mr. Bellow's brilliant book of 1964, *Herzog*, carries forward the basic design of his thought, morally and religiously—though here it is expressed far more with the extremely subtle indirection characteristic of *Seize the Day* than with the allegorical simplicity of *Henderson*. Moses Herzog is a forty-three-year-old Canadian Jew whose life has been spent sometimes in the midst of and sometimes on the fringes of academic circles in Chicago and

New York. He is an intellectual historian specializing in the Romantic movement, and his book, *Romanticism and Christianity*, though it never made a great splash, had, at the time of its appearance, established him as a young scholar of considerable originality and promise. But Herzog, bearing as he does a "great bone-breaking burden of selfhood," lacks some necessary gift for success. As the novel opens, his life appears very nearly to have collapsed into utter failure: he is without any academic portfolio; he has squandered a patrimony of twenty thousand dollars on the unredeemable dilapidation of an isolated country house in the Berkshires; he has been cuckolded by his best friend and deserted by Madeleine, the beautiful and malevolent bitch for whom he left his first wife Daisy; and his scholarly researches on Romanticism have reached an impasse, so that he has virtually given up his work on the book in progress. Indeed, the pressures of life have taken so heavy a toll that "some people thought he was cracked and for a time he himself had doubted that he was all there."

But then, at what seems to be the end of his tether, he begins to write letters—which are never posted—to his former mistresses and to General Eisenhower, to professional rivals and to his dead mother, to Adlai Stevenson and Martin Heidegger, to his first wife and to Friedrich Nietzsche, to contemporary British physicists and to Russian intellectuals of the nineteenth century, and "to everyone under the sun," even to God Himself. Through this discipline of letter writing—and through the recollection of the past and the sorting out of his experience that this discipline entails—Herzog undertakes to gather up and reorder the scattered fragments of his life. And the novel very largely consists of these letters—marvelously engrafted to the basic dramatic design—and of a plethora of flashbacks which gradually unfold the entire history of this man, by means of a *montage* whose execution is a beautifully dazzling feat of narration.

What is so engaging about this erratic and charming scapegrace, this representative mid-century "anti-hero," who takes a vain satisfaction in his slightly faded handsomeness and who is so inept at fending for himself in the rough and tumble of the world—what is so engaging about him is that, as he stands amidst the debris of his imprudent life, though he has constantly to resist the invading pressures of madness, he steadfastly refuses the "foolish dreariness" of "the Wasteland outlook." He has had his "schooling in grief," but he will not "tout" the Void; he knows enough about the whole Romantic experiment to understand that the modern fascination with the "florid extremism" of Crisis and Alienation leads nowhere but into what is only another blind alley. For all of his failures as scholar and lover and husband and father, he has no desire to contract out of history: so the "transcendence" that beckons for him is that which he finds the philosopher Jean Wahl calling "transcendence downwards." Our job, in other words, is not to get outside of life but to find within the human situation itself a redemptive center and a healing grace.

It is after the ending of his marriage with Madeleine that Moses begins to find a new steadiness and serenity. One day, being suddenly stirred by his love for their little daughter, he takes a plane from New York to Chicago, in order to pay her a visit. A friend in Chicago arranges with Madeleine for him to spend an afternoon with the child. And all goes well until, as he is returning June to her mother in a rented car, he becomes involved with another motorist in a minor collision. Since—for reasons fully explained in the narrative—he happens to have an unregistered revolver on his person, the policemen who come to the scene are required to "book" him: so June has to

accompany him to the precinct station. After Madeleine
has come for the child, as he faces his wife's motiveless
malignity and rage, he slowly begins really to see that the
brutal violence of this destructive woman has about it "a
fringe of insanity." Yet the very fire of her pointless
malevolence has a certain purgative effect, for it elicits
from him an inward act of rejection. He knows that he
owes the powers that created him "a human life," and he
makes us feel the dawning realization in himself that living
"a human life" involves, however quietly and unobtru-
sively, the making of a sort of testimony—not to apocalypse and crisis and alienation, but in behalf of the "ordinary middling human considerations." So he goes back to
his house in the Berkshires, there at last to bring his
letter-writing to an end and, like Candide, to begin to
cultivate his garden, with the beautiful Castilian Ramona
Donsell, a successful New York businesswoman, who
adores him and for whose robust sensuality and delicious
Shrimp Arnaud he has a fine appetite.

But, though Mr. Bellow's story is a story of salvation
and of Paradise Regained and though Herzog's letters are
dense with a very sophisticated kind of commentary on
the lore and ideology of modern intellectual life (recalling
in this respect the Mann of *Der Zauberberg and Doktor
Faustus*), the novel is in no way a solemn morality. It is
drenched in a fun and lightheartedness and wit which have
that very Jewish sort of bounce and rhythm by which *The
Adventures of Augie March* is so marked. And the gaiety
and playfulness that give raciness to Mr. Bellow's language
and *élan* to his deployment of character and situation are a
part of what is substantive in his message: he wants to
convey a most stringent judgment of that *Angst*-ridden
mentality which has for so long been our fashionable mode
of seriousness, and he wants to suggest that there is healing
in laughter. Indeed, the comedy of *Herzog* is a comedy of

redemption, and of a redemption whose catalyst is of the same sort as that which initiates the process of restoration in Mr. Bellow's earlier books—namely, the quitting of anxiety, of stress, of struggle. For Moses begins to hear "indefinite music within" and to be on his way towards blessedness once he decides "to surrender the hyperactivity of this hyperactive face. . . . just to put it out instead to the radiance of the sun." Then it is that a new peace settles over the novel, as he, in the final chapter—now back at his property in the Berkshires—begins to paint a piano for little June and walks quietly in the woods and makes arrangements with a local cleaning woman to put his house in order. "Whatever had come over him during these last months, the spell really seemed to be passing, really going." Indeed, the time even comes when he gives up his letter writing. "Yes, that was what was coming, in fact. The knowledge that he was done with these letters." For, now "feeling that he was easily contained by everything about him," he has "no messages for anyone else. . . . Not a single word." By returning and rest and quietness, he is brought—by Grace—into a new domain of the spirit, where it is good to be, since here (as St. Bernard says) a man

> . . . . . . . . . . . . vivit purius,
> Cadit rarius, surgit velocius, incedit cautius,
> Quiescit securius, moritur felicius,
> Purgatur citius, proemiatur copiosus.

\*       \*       \*

It may well be the constant deepening over the past twenty years of Mr. Bellow's conviction that the way into blessedness and felicity is the way of what Martin Heidegger calls *Gelassenheit*,[16] of acquiescent submission to the

[16]See Martin Heidegger, *Gelassenheit* (Pfullingen: Günther Neske Verlag, 1959).

multileveled and radical mystery of existence, the way of *falling*-into Peace—it may well be his deepening commitment to the Blakean abjuration of "braces," with all the scepticism it implies about the redemptive power of *action*, that in large measure accounts for the steadily increasing tendency of his fiction to expend its major energies in an essentially meditative enterprise. As we move from *Dangling Man* to *Henderson* and from *The Victim* to *Herzog*, his heroes seem more and more to be cast in the role of brooding *penseur*, and what is recounted in the way of incident strikes us as largely but "a way of interrupting the hero's reflections"—on, as Alfred Kazin says, "the root of all creation."[17] Which is perhaps why, in its penchant for a large kind of exploratory rumination, Mr. Bellow's fiction needs the spaciousness of the novel and does not normally find its happiest expressions in the shorter forms of narrative. The volume of his stories published in 1968 under the title *Mosby's Memoirs* is, in all its parts, marked by the trenchancy of moral intelligence, the dexterity in *montage*, and the brilliance of language that are now expected regularly to distinguish his style of performance as a writer. In two memorable instances—"Leaving the Yellow House" (about a cheerful, bibulous old lady in the Utah desert trying desperately to hold on to her yellow house which is her last means of independence) and "Looking for Mr. Green" (about a white caseworker whose job it is to deliver relief checks in a Chicago black ghetto)—the *agonia* being recorded throbs with the ache of those who know how large a part catastrophe plays in the life of the soul. But the general impression of his readers is likely to be that the kind of work presented in his book of 1968 does not represent his natural métier, and that his

[17]Alfred Kazin, "Though He Slay Me . . . ," *The New York Review of Books*, 15, no. 10 (3 December 1970): 3.

gifts are most fully engaged only when he allows himself the kind of room in which to move about that the longer forms of fiction provide.

In the novel which appeared in 1970, *Mr. Sammler's Planet*, Mr. Bellow is, however, once again in his proper element, and the book marks one of the major achievements of his career, particularly in the evidence it affords that the way of *Gelassenheit* does not for him entail any abdication from the social contract, or from the moral requirements arising out of the fact that the fundamental setting of human life is always the *Polis*, the reality of our fellowmanhood.

The time of the novel is that dark moment of the late 1960s, when, as it seemed, the new period-style in political and cultural life was beginning to be a kind of casual nihilism whose hallmark was the great impatience with the past, that easy contempt for the disciplines of reason, that surly refusal of the civilities of liberal democracy being expressed by the new shoving, badgering *enragés* with their cries of "Up against the wall. . . ." The place is New York City, more particularly that dreary, dingy world of New York's Upper West Side which Mr. Bellow had masterfully charted in *Seize the Day*, as the representative site of the contemporary megalopolitan's unease. It is against this background that he places his protagonist, a courtly and cultivated old Polish Jew now in his seventies, Artur Sammler, widowed survivor of a Nazi death pit, who, after his escape from that place of carnage, did by his own hand murder a German soldier in the Zamosht Forest, with a pleasure which itself brought the recognition that has since constituted the great burden of his life, "that reality was a terrible thing, and the final truth about mankind overwhelming and crushing."

The New York scene of the sixties surrounds him, however, with people so bereft of ancient memories, so captive to the new antinomianism and so unpracticed in the habit of reflection that the special slant of his moral perceptions makes Sammler very much of an *isolé*. Margotte, the niece with whom he lives in her large and untidy Ninetieth Street apartment, staves off the emptiness created by the loss of her husband (a Hunter College professor killed in a plane crash) with high-minded, tedious discussions and speculations and arguments and explanations, with *"Weimar schmaltz"* about the Banality of Evil and the role of technics in Modern Civilization and various other "big" questions (Creativity, the Young, the Blacks, the Victims): in her world there is very little light and a great deal of clutter.

"But when it came to clutter, his daughter, Shula, was much worse." Turned out in miniskirts "revealing legs sensual in outline but without inner sensuality" and wearing "on her head a wig such as a female impersonator might put on at a convention of salesmen," she is a passionate collector who, with her shopping bags, strays along upper Broadway, foraging for whatever may happen to attract her in streetcorner trash baskets—as she also loonily forages amongst the city's temples and synagogues and auditoriums for the cheering slogans and catchwords that may be looted from sermons and free lectures. This half-mad but harmless creature, with her floridly painted lips and her kinky hair descending from the absurd wig, lives apart from her equally batty husband, Eisen, an Israeli painter, who is, like his father-in-law, a survivor of the German holocaust, but one for whom the horrors of history are no longer the terribly repellent reality they are for Sammler. Indeed, Eisen now puts "the divinity of art" at the service of outrage, painting the human image as an image not of life but of death—and, once he arrives in the States, this daft personage, with his moist and perfect little teeth, can only talk greedily of his hunger for a successful career (which he calls *karyera*).

Or, again, there is Angela, the daughter of Sammler's

wealthy nephew and benefactor, Dr. Elya Gruner—"one of those handsome, passionate, rich girls" who make by themselves "an important social and human category"; one who got a characteristically bad American education at Sarah Lawrence; a young woman whose soul is fed by her psychiatrist and Andy Warhol and The Living Theatre and minimal painting and the Beatles; who spends her days training in a fashionable gymnasium for the rigors of the various affairs and exotic group scenes to which her nights are devoted. "In Angela you confronted sensual womanhood without remission. You smelled it, too." And her brother, Wallace, is a "high I.Q. moron" who has practiced law briefly but whose eagerness to win a fortune of his own and independence from his father places him at the mercy of every harebrained scheme which is proposed to him: so he simply drifts, maladroitly, from one misadventure to another—having nearly become a physicist, a mathematician, "nearly a lawyer . . . , nearly an engineer, nearly a Ph.D. in behavioral science. . . . Nearly an alcoholic, nearly a homosexual," and now being at the point of very nearly becoming a specialist in the handicapping of professional football scores. "A young man with stunning gifts."

Wallace's friend, Lionel Feffer, is not ineligible for their relationship, for he, too, is hunting some piece of turf that will be his to exploit and enjoy. He is a young man without allegiances or commitments, a *déraciné*, who, as a Columbia graduate student, arranges for Sammler to address a seminar in which he is enrolled. The old gentleman is a great Anglophile who, many years earlier, as a correspondent in London, had come to feel a deep affection for the special graces and stabilities of English life, so much so that, through his friendship with people like H. G. Wells and the various princelings of Bloomsbury, he became as one to that stream of culture born, a sort of Polish Oxonian. And thus young Feffer—whose conversation ("like any page of Joyce's *Ulysses,* always *in medias res"*) is always a chaotic affair of scandals and cross references and of his many schemes and projects, and who has a great zest for promoting a scene—proposes that Mr. Sammler address the seminar on "the British Scene in the Thirties." So Sammler accompanies him to the campus one afternoon, expecting "to reminisce, for a handful of interested students," about the atmosphere of English politics and culture in the years *entre deux guerres,* about Oswald Mosley and the Peoples' Front and John Strachey, about R. H. Tawney and Harold Laski and George Orwell. But instead of entering a small seminar room, he is ushered into a crowded amphitheatre where he finds himself facing "a large, spreading, shaggy, composite human bloom" that gives off an air "malodorous, peculiarly rancid, sulphurous." His erudite recollections and ironies are not well received by this audience, and when, at a certain point, he speaks of George Orwell's having remarked the protection afforded British radicals by the Royal Navy, he is loudly interrupted by a bearded, Levi-clad young person who shouts at him: "Hey! Old Man! . . . . That's a lot of shit. Orwell was a fink. . . . It's good he died when he did." Furthermore, he is told by this *furieux* that he is himself an "effete old shit" who "can't come" because his "balls are dry." And, as he leaves the hall, he is "not so much personally offended by the event" as he is struck by how much the radical young—with their extraordinary minglings of explosiveness and "sex-excrement-militancy"—are moved by a passion not only to be *real* but also to be brutal and to offend.

So, facing the hysteria and *anomie* of the strange Wasteland indwelt by his relatives and their friends and all the various human flotsam he meets on the streets of the Upper West Side, it is no wonder that this good old European—who, in his meditations on Tauler and Meister Eckhart, on Kant and Max Scheler, on Burckhardt and

Freud, on Baudelaire and Max Weber, bears the full weight
of his spiritual inheritance—it is no wonder that he feels
"somewhat separated from the rest of his species." Amidst
the noisy, vulgar violence and flamboyant crudity of the
American 1960s, he feels "severed" from the time not so
much by his advanced age as by "preoccupations too
different and remote" to be compatible with the new
dispensation, so different indeed as to give him a sense of
being touched in his own person by something like the
kind of vulnerability belonging to a man cast by Henry
Moore, full of holes and gaps.

Sammler is not, however, without sympathies. He
comes, for example, to have a certain fellow-feeling for an
extraordinary person who operates as a pickpocket on
Riverside Drive buses—a huge, elegantly dressed Negro
decked out in smoked glasses by Christian Dior, his "powerful throat banded by a tab collar and a cherry silk
necktie," and his stylish camel's-hair coat giving off the
scent of French perfume. It is with a marvelous nimbleness
that this big black dandy carries his furled English umbrella in one hand, while, with the polished forefinger of the
other hand, rifling wallets and purses, turning aside the
plastic folders with Social Security and credit cards till he
comes to "the green of money." And on each occasion of
his finding this brilliant figure on his bus, as he rides
uptown from the Forty-Second Street Library, Mr. Sammler is enormously quickened by the consummate artistry of
his performance. "It was a powerful event, and illicitly—
that is, against his own stable principles—he craved a repetition." So fascinated, indeed, does he become that finally
he attracts the Negro's attention. And one afternoon the
pickpocket follows him home: as soon as the old man
enters the empty lobby of his building, he is grabbed and
thrust against the wall. "What is the matter? What do you
want?" Sammler cries out. But the black man says not a

word. As he holds his prey with one great fist, he reaches
into his trousers with his other hand and takes out his
"large tan-and-purple uncircumcised" penis—which he simply shows to his elderly captive, with a serenely candid
lordliness and a strangely "mystifying certitude." Then he
releases Sammler, closes his fly, smoothes his streaming
silk necktie, picks up his umbrella, and departs, having said
in effect, with a splended kind of hauteur: "Old man,
don't mess with me."

In its immediate effect, the encounter is of course
deeply unsettling for Mr. Sammler. But gradually there
comes a time when he realizes that, though a certain
madness no doubt lurks behind this gorgeous dandy's
"barbarous-majestical manner," what he is "mad with [is]
an idea of noblesse": his way of reckoning with "the
slackness and cowardice of the world," for all of its outrageous freebootery, does, nevertheless, express an imperi-
ousness of humanity for which Sammler cannot help feeling a profound sympathy. He recognizes a certain bond of
kinship between himself and this black thief, for they are
both outsiders. And he is moved by something like admiration for the brigand's intention to *survive*. But to Wallace
Gruner and young Feffer the Negro pickpocket's "serenely
masterful" exultation in his own adroitness and potency
simply invites an aggressive kind of curiosity and an impulse to assault. With the "scientific objectivity" of a
"high I.Q. moron," Wallace is eager to get from Sammler
the most exact possible estimates of the Negro's tool—"It
wasn't actually black, was it? It must have been a purple
kind of chocolate, or maybe the color of his palms?
. . . . Would you guess it weighed two pounds, three
pounds, four? . . . . Uncircumcised? . . . . What else did the
man do, did he shake the thing at you?" And Feffer wants
to put his little Minox camera to work: he wants to get
some pictures of the pickpocket in action which can then

be sold to a magazine. The Negro, understandably, is unwilling to cooperate with this scheme: so, at the time of the photographic attack, he struggles with Feffer for the camera, and a fight ensues. Sammler begs Eisen to separate them and to give the camera to the thief—but instead his son-in-law aims a series of crushing blows at the black man's face with a bag of iron medallions he is carrying. And what Sammler is horrified by is not the pickpocket but the meddling, greedy malignity of Feffer and the heartless brutality of the madman from Haifa.

It is not only the nameless Negro, however, who claims Mr. Sammler's sympathy. Despite the radical divergence in their views of the world, he also comes to feel a very deep affinity of interest and concern between himself and a brilliant Hindu biophysicist who lectures at Columbia, Dr. V. Govinda Lal. Dr. Lal has recently completed a monograph which is yet to be published, on "The Future of the Moon," and its opening sentence immediately suggests something of the kind of scientifically based eschatology to which he is committed—"How long will this earth remain the only home of Man?" He is quick to admit that he does not have "the full blueprint" of the coming age, but he is unshakably confident that the new expeditions into outer space open up a fresh alternative for human destiny; and one of the novel's great moments is the long dialogue on this question between him and Mr. Sammler.

"Not to go where one can go may be stunting": this is one of Dr. Lal's fundamental axioms. And the matter, he feels, is given a special urgency in our time by the "surplus of humanity" on the face of the earth. "We are crowded in, packed in," so much so that we have arrived at a stage in the evolution of the race when "we cannot manage with one single planet," for "the species is eating itself up." Indeed, not to accept the new opportunities presented by aeronautical science for "earth-departure" and for colonizing other worlds would be to "make this earth seem more and more a prison," most especially now that "Kingdom Come is directly over us waiting to receive" us. "Much better the moon."

Mr. Sammler, however, is without any instinct for "leaping into Kingdom Come." This cultivated old European has no *goût* for apocalyptic enterprise: he takes it for granted that this world, conditioned and limited and unsatisfactory as it most assuredly is, is the only world truly at man's disposal and that one must, therefore, undertake to reckon with it—"whatever inner reservations," as he says, "truth imposes." Little Dr. Lal—"hunched, dusky, with his rusty-gilt complexion, his full face and beard"—is unwilling to treat with "the present state of affairs": he wants humanity to hurl itself toward some new planet. But Sammler suspects that this passion for the colonization of other worlds may be only the latest expression of that "peculiar longing for nonbeing" which recurrently seizes the modern imagination; and, though he also suspects that our sheer fascination with engineering projects will doubtless in due time prompt us to attempt the colonizing of outer space, his own preference, as he says, would be that we seek "to have justice on this planet first." Yet, though he sees Lal as "an Eastern curiosity . . . mentally rebounding from limits like a horsefly from glass," he is charmed by the little man, for, as he thinks, "His conversation was conversation, it was not a line. This was no charlatan, only an oddity."

But Mr. Sammler's deepest sympathies are claimed by his nephew, Dr. Elya Gruner, in whose head there is "a great blood vessel, defective from birth, worn thin and frayed with a lifetime of pulsation." And, as a result of this aneurysm, Gruner is now dying. He has acquired all the accouterments of the large success he has enjoyed in New York as a gynecologist—a socially prominent wife

(now dead), a great house in Westchester County, a magnificent Rolls Royce, "glittering like a silver tureen." Yet
he is a man of unrequited longings, made especially bitter
in his last days by the ingratitude and heartless inattention
of his two handsome, worthless children (Angela and Wallace). He is not, of course, himself unflawed, and his great
wealth has been gained by more than a little sharp practice. Wallace, for example, is certain that vast sums of
money his father has gathered in fees for abortions from
New York *mafiosi* are cached away in his house. And as
Gruner lies dying in his hospital room this hustling young
trickster is ravenously ripping out plumbing fixtures in
which he believes the money to be concealed. But, though
Gruner is far from representing any sort of heroic virtue,
Sammler knows him to be a decent man, one whose
fidelity to his ancestral community in Israel and whose
quiet kindliness and generosity toward his family and his
friends make him deserve indeed in the ordinary scales of
life to be considered a good man. It was Gruner who
brought him and Shula to the States after the War and who
has supported them ever since, paying their rents and
inventing work for Shula and supplementing German in-
demnity checks (which he was at great pains, through his
lawyers, to arrange). Sammler knows, of course, that his
nephew is rich and can easily afford these charities, but he
also knows that the rich are usually mean, being unable to
put aside the "infighting, habitual fraud, [the] mad agility
in compound deceit," by which they have made their
money. "Sammler knew the defects of his man. Saw them
as dust and pebbles, as rubble on a mosaic which might be
swept away. Underneath, a fine, noble expression. A de-
pendable man—a man who took thought for others." So he
loves his nephew who, however imperfect he may be, has
never failed in solicitude and liberality and who has constantly kept faith with him. As the old man says at

Gruner's bedside, "You've been good to Shula and me, Elya." And thus he wants to help the dying man to have a good death and to bring him such comfort as he can be given in the hour of his life's last great emergency.

Not even the old gentleman, however, with all of his stern rectitude, can manage to elicit any compassion or tenderness for their dying father from Wallace and Angela. The son is busy taking apart the pipes in his father's house, and the daughter is wholly preoccupied with complications that have arisen in her relationship with her latest paramour. When Sammler begs her to offer some reconciling and affectionate word to her father before the end, she says: "What do you have in mind? . . . . What do you want from me? . . . . As far as I can see . . . you want an old-time deathbed scene." To which he is moved to reply:

> "I only note the peculiarity that it is possible to be gay, amorous, intimate with holiday acquaintances. Diversions, group intercourse, fellatio with strangers— one can do that but not come to terms with one's father at the last opportunity."

So it is Sammler alone who is left to keep watch over the bedside. And, at the last, as he looks down at the dead man and notices how "bitterness and an expression of obedience" are combined in his lips, he offers up the deeply felt requiem with which the novel comes to a close:

> "Remember, God, the soul of Elya Gruner, who, as willingly as possible and as well as he was able, and even to an intolerable point, and even in suffocation and even as death was coming was eager, even childishly perhaps (may I be forgiven for this), even with a certain servility, to do what was required of him. At his best this man was much kinder than at my very best I have ever been or could ever be. He was aware that he must meet, and

he did meet—through all the confusion and degraded
clowning of this life through which we are speeding—he
did meet the terms of his contract. The terms which, in
his inmost heart, each man knows. As I know mine. As
all know. For that is the truth of it—that we all know,
God, that we know, that we know, we know, we
know."

Quite apart from the extraordinary distinction of intelligence and brilliance of wit with which *Mr. Sammler's
Planet* defines its adversary position vis-à-vis the moral
bedlam of the American 1960s, the book, when considered
not only in terms of its own singular profundity but also in
its relation to the entire *oeuvre* to which it belongs, must
be felt to have a very considerable importance. For it
makes powerfully evident what many of Mr. Bellow's
readers may have previously failed to notice—namely, that
the commitment of his fiction to something like a principle of *sola gratia* has in no way inclined it toward any
scanting or disregard of the moral imperatives wrought
into the fibre of our fellowmanhood. The account of
human existence which his fiction projects does not, in
other words, propose any short cuts to ecstasy; and he
very much wants to counterbalance the testimony that the
"axial lines" of life become discernible "when striving
stops" with the kind of witness in whose behalf Artur
Sammler desires most passionately to present his own
affidavit—that, implicit in our human condition, there is a
sort of "contract" with the Thou, and one the breach of
which must (in its dishonoring of "the sacrament of the
brother"[18] ) diminish what men have together around that
campfire that staves off the dark wilderness beyond.

[18]The phrase is Hans Urs von Balthasar's: see his *Science, Religion
and Christianity*, trans. by Hilda Graef (Westminster, Md.: Newman
Press, 1958), pp. 142-55.

"Choose dignity," says old Schlossberg in *The Victim*. And the protagonist of that novel, Asa Leventhal, does not escape at the last the recognition that the idea of the " 'human' [means being] accountable in spite of many weaknesses"—which is to say what Augie March wants to insist upon: namely, "this universal eligibility to be noble." Nor does that "indefinite music within" by which Moses Herzog is finally stirred fail to include as one of its themes an intention "to share with other human beings" whatever it may be that is granted of grace and opportunity. And it is a similar avowal of the "human bond" that Mr. Bellow's fiction is recurrently seeking to express, for it does not want to be a literature of Negative Capability.

He knows, of course, that he is striking against many of the strongest head winds of the age, that one of the deepest assumptions of modern literary intelligence is that "the pursuit of the positive" is bound to have a blighting effect on literary art. Indeed, in one of his essays he undertakes quite straightforwardly to meet the contention (as expressed by Leslie Fiedler) that it is the duty of the writer always to be in the ranks of the Opposition and always to say "No! in thunder." Mr. Bellow wants in reply, however, to insist that "the idiocy of orthodox affirmation and transparent or pointless optimism ought not to provoke an equal and opposite reaction."[19] Furthermore, as he says, "either we want life to continue or we do not. If we don't want [it] to continue, why write books? The wish for death is powerful and silent. It . . . has no need of words." And "if we answer yes, we do want [life] . . . to continue, [then] we are liable to be asked how. In what form shall life be justified?"[20]

[19]Saul Bellow, "The Writer as Moralist," *The Atlantic Monthly*, 211, no. 3 (March, 1963): 61.
[20]*Ibid.*, p. 62.

Now it is his profound engagement with this question that not only establishes the moral center of his work but that also prompts the voice one regularly hears behind the scenes of his fiction to adopt the peculiar kind of double tone that has come to be so familiarly distinctive of Saul Bellow's style. For, given his great unabashed didactic propensity and the consequent necessity he has faced of fashioning a speech limber and sprightly enough to keep us from responding to its deliverances as merely an affair of preachment, his chosen strategem has been one, as Irving Howe has remarked, of mingling "two narrative voices ..., the first sententious and the second sardonic, yet with the declamations of the sententious voice never quite undone, and sometimes even slyly reinforced, by the thrusts of the sardonic voice." The "smoke screens of elaborate comic rhetoric" (comprised at once of "demotic richness [and] ... mandarin eloquence, racy-tough street Jewishness [and] ... high-flown intellectual display"[21] ) have never effectively concealed his seriousness of purpose, but his insistently didactic intention has had the effect of making rhetoric itself—rather than action and character— the main source of the essential energies in his fiction. And there is perhaps no other comparable body of work in the literature of the contemporary novel so drenched in ideas and speculations and theories, even commandments. Yet the marvel of his books is that the musings and cogitations of Augie March and Moses Herzog and Artur Sammler are so brilliantly rendered as data for "direct sensuous apprehension" that (to borrow a famous line of T. S. Eliot's) we "feel their thought as immediately as the odor of a rose."[22]

21Irving Howe, "Fiction: Bellow, O'Hara, Litwak," *Harper's Magazine*, 240, no. 1437 (February, 1970): 106.
22T. S. Eliot, "The Metaphysical Poets," in *Selected Essays: 1917-1932* (New York: Harcourt, Brace and Co., 1932), p. 247.

Many years ago, it is true—in the passage quoted earlier on from the "Address by Gooley MacDowell to the Has-beens Club of Chicago"—Mr. Bellow recorded his belief that today we suffer from a surfeit of "wise counsel and good precept," and so indeed we may. But the wise counsel of which there may be too much is that which presents itself in the form of the bloodless abstraction, the humanly discarnate generality—and one suspects that the witty eloquence with which his fiction manages to pierce our spirit's sleep is, in its great power to enliven the moral imagination, something as rare today as it has always been.

# Lionel Trilling's Anxious Humanism - The Search for "Authenticity"

# IV

# Lionel Trilling's
# Anxious Humanism -
# The Search for "Authenticity"

Though it was with an increasing frequency that Lionel
Trilling's articles and reviews made their appearance
through the 1930s and though his Columbia doctoral dissertation on Matthew Arnold, immediately after its publication in 1939, established itself as the definitive contemporary account of Arnold's career,[1] the onset of his own
career—as a major presence in American literary life—is to
be dated in the mid-1940's. For it was in those years that
he began to issue (most often in *Partisan Review* and *The
Kenyon Review*) the remarkable essays which, as they have
since continued at intervals to appear and then to be
anthologized in the various collections he has arranged of
his work, now constitute one of the great and beautiful
achievements of the American literary intelligence in our
time. He has, in short, over the span of nearly a generation
been a commanding figure in the national House of Intellect. In a period when criticism (in the manner, say, of a
Richard Poirier or a Leslie Fiedler) is busily engaged with

[1]See Lionel Trilling, *Matthew Arnold* (New York: W. W. Norton &
Co., 1939; rev. ed., New York: Columbia University Press, 1949).

153

that region of things belonging to the new "popular" culture—the Beatles-and-all-that—or when (in the manner of a Susan Sontag) it is declaring criticism to be itself a vicious betrayal of art, university students and their younger teachers are not, of course, so readily inclined as at an earlier time to reckon with a mind such as Mr. Trilling's that takes a very large delight in the vivacious complexities of which a vigorous and self-confident criticism is capable. Indeed, given the present slump of our cultural life—towards the lunacies of what Saul Bellow calls "an amusement society"[2]—one's impression is that Mr. Trilling's books, like so much else of weight and merit in the recent past, do not now claim quite so large a measure of prestige as they did a decade or more ago. But, for all the distance at which the graceful civility of its idiom may stand from the slangy chic of newly modish critical parlances, his is a body of work which does still splendidly bring into focus the nub of that central perplexity which is felt by the people whose placement in history has permitted them to be deeply affected by the legacy of Rousseau and Marx and Freud. And thus he makes a kind of *exemplum* which, in some small degree perhaps, we fail to contemplate at our peril.

Some notice has, of course, occasionally been taken of the anomaly that Mr. Trilling represented on the literary scene of the period, say, between the late forties and the early sixties, when his reputation was in the fullest tide of its glory. For, in those years, most of the reigning figures in the forums of Anglo-American criticism kept as their principal commitment that very strenuous exegetical enterprise of verbal analysis and "explication" of literary structure that made them the New Critics John Crowe Ransom

[2]Saul Bellow, "Culture Now: Some Animadversions, Some Laughs," *Modern Occasions*, 1, no. 2 (Winter, 1971): 178.

declared them to be, in his book of 1941 (*The New Criticism*) which gave the movement its name and its first major advertisement. The harvest gathered by the New Criticism, in its American phase, is perhaps most typically exemplified by two of its finest products—Cleanth Brooks's *The Well Wrought Urn* (1947) and Reuben Brower's *The Fields of Light* (1951). In these books, one is being invited to participate in what is a most strenuous effort indeed, of descrying (by means of the closest possible study of "design," of "tenor" and "vehicle," of tension and ambiguity and symbolic action) wherein the given work of art is an object of knowledge *sui generis*. It was in such a search—for that irreducible identity of "structure" whereby the particular poem or novel manages to be exactly what it is and not another thing—that the most representative people of Mr. Trilling's generation found the burden they felt required to assume. And it was this common commitment which engendered that characteristic style of critical performance we recognize today in the work of such critics as R. P. Blackmur, Mark Schorer, Allen Tate, Robert Heilman, and Dorothy Van Ghent.

Lionel Trilling's position, however, was always noticeably outside this circle. For, as he has said (in the essay "On the Teaching of Modern Literature" in *Beyond Culture*), his interests have consistently led him

> . . . to see literary situations as cultural situations, and cultural situations as great elaborate fights about moral issues, and moral issues as having something to do with gratuitously chosen images of personal being, and images of personal being as having something to do with literary style. . . .

It is precisely in this complex dialectical pattern—of the self and the moral life, of literature and culture—that all his critical work has found its leading focus. Indeed, it is his having elected to address himself most principally, like Schiller and Coleridge and Arnold, to what literature *does* rather than merely to what it *is*,[3] and it is the extraordinary brilliance with which his thought has proceeded in this dimension, that no doubt largely accounts for his having borne, as a man of letters, such an Emersonian centrality for those who entered adulthood between 1939 and the mid-'forties as no American intellectual other than perhaps the late Reinhold Niebuhr has commanded. And many suspect now that, for all the "impurity" of his criticism, it may well stand a better chance of surviving over, say, the next hundred years than that of any other American of our period (with the exception, possibly, of portions of Edmund Wilson's work and of F. O. Matthiessen's pioneering masterpiece, *American Renaissance*). For, however useful may be that clerkly patience which spends itself on teaching us how rightly to discern the internality of a work of art—and we must all surely find it indispensable—it does not satisfy the ultimate demand of the mind, which is that ways shall be found, once the poem has done its full work upon us, of bringing our experience of it into some significant relationship with the generality of cultural forms and meanings. And the critics—like Marcel Raymond and Erich Heller and F. R. Leavis and Lionel Trilling—who offer some help in this way are likely to be regarded, finally, as the most valuable, especially when they command the high rhetorical gifts these men possess.

\*       \*       \*

Judged against our contemporary standard—which is far less absolute than its "true believers" generally realize—Mr.

[3]I have borrowed this distinction from the late Willian Van O'Connor: see his "Lionel Trillings's Critical Realism," *The Sewanee Review*, 58, no. 3 (July-September, 1950): 490-91.

Trilling's criticism must, it is true, be acknowledged as more than a little "impure." For his interests have most assuredly led him to see literary situations as cultural and moral situations, so much so indeed that he sometimes makes us feel that he—no doubt not in any very highly conscious or programmatic way—regards criticism as a department of philosophy and as most particularly related to that specific philosophical discipline which, by reason of its special concern with the nature and place and prospect of man, is known, in its traditional designation, as "anthropology." Yet, despite the consistency with which the critical act for him has made an occasion for an essentially anthropological inquiry—despite the unfailing intensity of his long meditation on the exigencies attendant upon the life of selfhood in the modern world—what cannot fail to be immediately remarked is that, nevertheless, unlike so many others of his generation in criticism (the late F. O. Matthiessen, Allen Tate, Cleanth Brooks, W. K. Wimsatt), his thought has never embraced any sort of religious position. One even feels a primary effort of his mind to be one which has been spent in firmly and constantly resolving that the question of man shall remain an anthropological question and shall never be permitted to elevate itself into the precincts of metaphysics or theology. Mr. Trilling has, in short, always shown himself to be a thinker most determinedly committed to a secular perspective. Here is perhaps the most decisive characteristic of his fundamental position, and, in this respect, it may be the fine novel which he published in 1947, *The Middle of the Journey*, that, of all his writings, most immediately discloses the general atmosphere of his mind.

The milieu of *The Middle of the Journey* is that of the American literary and political intelligentsia at mid-century, and there are five people whom the novel presents as the chief exemplars of its constituency. First, there is John

Laskell—"a fortunate young man of the middle class" for whom the world "might perhaps have absorbing doubts but certainly not any fears"; one who takes life in the sensible, solicitous ways of a generous liberalism; who, with an impressive book recently out, is beginning to win a solid reputation as an authority on urban housing; but who, for all his skeptical maturity, is, in his thirty-third year, at that difficult Dantean juncture—*nel mezzo del cammin*—where the self begins to feel the pressures of fate and destiny.

Laskell's most cherished friends are Nancy and Arthur Croom. Arthur, a young university economist, has also, like Laskell himself, been brought to the threshold of large professional recognition by a recently published book on business cycles. He, too, writes for liberal magazines, lives on the fringes of radical politics. And, in their "passionate expectation of the future," in their sturdy commitment to justice and decency and the promotion of reason in the large affairs of public life, Arthur and his charming wife Nancy have come to be affectionately regarded by Laskell as a kind of "justification of human existence."

Then there are two others, known at once by Laskell and the Crooms—Kermit Simpson, the wealthy publisher of a liberal magazine, *The New Era*, that sponsors leftist causes; and Gifford Maxim, long an underground agent of "the Party," "a man of the far future, the bloody, moral, apocalyptic future that was sure to come," whose ascetic purity of dedication to the world of Tomorrow has become for such people as Laskell and the Crooms something like a touchstone wherewith their own less extreme and more prudential allegiances are to be most severely judged.

Now it is in a late summer month that these five persons are drawn into the quiet and crucial drama the novel recounts. Laskell has just barely survived a grave illness. And, with his nurses now dismissed, he is at the point of closing his New York apartment and going to the Crooms' summer residence in the Connecticut valley for a few weeks of convalescence, when Maxim appears—to announce his defection from "the Party" and his consequent fear of assassination. He wants Laskell to persuade Kermit Simpson to grant him a position on the staff of Simpson's dim little magazine, for, given the absolute obscurity in which he has lived over the past year of his underground work, he is convinced that he can remain alive now only by recovering a public identity. "I must have a continuous existence, an office I go to every day, so that it is perfectly clear that if one day I don't appear, questions will be asked. I must be on record to be safe. I want my existence established on, say, the masthead of *The New Era*. The more I exist and the more I exist publicly, the safer I am." So, with some reluctance, Laskell rings up Simpson at his summer house in Westport and persuades him to offer Maxim an assistant editorship.

But, for all the distaste provoked in him by his friend's reversal, Laskell's own situation is not wholly unlike Maxim's, for he, too, has come to a point of needing to find new bearings. His illness has entailed a strange and nearly inarticulable experience of discovery, for it has somehow awakened in him the barely conscious surmise of what may be the inadequacy of his moderate liberal faith to the ultimate emergencies—of suffering and anxiety and death—by which the self is assailable. Indeed, one of his nurses had noticed after a time how great a "love affair" he was having with a certain flower in his room, a beautifully tawny pink rose in a vase on his bed-table; and he is astonished now by his faint suspicion that the static perfection of that flower figured forth the peace of a kind of nirvana and that, in his defenselessness and infirmity, he was perhaps embracing death.

None of this, however, as he learns, is it possible to talk

about with Nancy and Arthur, after he settles in down the road from their little cottage with a family in whose house the Crooms have arranged for him to stay. Illness and death are simply beyond their powers of thought. Indeed, to permit such facts to have any status in the clear, optimistic, rational world of modern people would be for them, they make us feel, to endorse a *politically* reactionary position: which is to say that, in their sense of things, it would be in that order of impropriety requiring to be considered as sinful. So their warm, deep affection for Laskell prompts them to cluck over him tenderly and solicitously: they take him in and cherish him, and, as day follows day, they talk endlessly together about their work and their friends and the various public affairs in which they take a common interest. But whenever he tries to speak of what it was like to be sick and very nearly to have died, they withdraw themselves "in a polite, intelligent, concerted way . . . as if they were the parents of a little boy and were following the line of giving no heed to the obscenities their son picked up on the street and insisted on bringing to the dinner table. . . . They simply, in a sensible modern way, paid no attention at all."

Nor is their incompetence in relation to the experience Laskell has recently undergone unrelated to their way of responding to their handyman, Duck Caldwell. Though descended from a once important Connecticut family, the line has by him been brought to the level of virtual indigence. And Duck, in his languid shiftlessness, by reluctantly taking on occasional odd jobs in the neighborhood only just barely succeeds in providing a very minimal support for his wife and little daughter. He is an unreliable, coarsely salacious, alcoholic malapert—not wicked, in any large or dangerous way, but simply captive to "the pure will of nothingness." His wife Emily, however, is a different quantity. Her anachronistic bohemianism, her "vague gentilities," the foolish articulations of her intellect (as when she chirps about how "wonderful" Spengler is)—all this is something mildly absurd. But Emily is not wholly defined by her inaptitude for being either an intellectual or a rebel. For, in her role as the mother of her vivacious little daughter Susan, in "her worry about Susan's education, in her function as housekeeper with her little prides in the midst of poverty, in her not at all striking talk about ordinary things," she has, as Laskell comes to realize, "a womanly dignity that [does] ... not depend on intellect—a kind of biological intelligence." But, despite their principled largemindedness toward the lower classes, the Crooms do not see this, for theirs is a highly abstract benevolence that leads them to consider the Caldwells not in a personal way but as examples of their *kind*. And since Emily's essential integrity and good sense do not make so large a claim on their generosity as Duck's shiftiness and unreliability, Nancy and Arthur make Emily's *gaucheries* the object of their malice, while Duck, whom they talk about incessantly and happily, is for them "a high manifestation of ordinary life." They tell Laskell that Duck has "his own way of doing things and ... can't be hurried." Which leads him to wonder how it comes to be that his liberal, progressive friends who want to hurry so many other manifestations of reality yet find it possible to provide a kind of exemption for this devious scapegrace.

Laskell knows, of course, that it would be extravagant to think of Duck as an agent of "evil." But he feels him certainly to be ineligible for the role assigned him by the Crooms, of being—by reason of his manual skills and his racy speech and his poverty—a symbol of something vaguely noble and good. And it is some unformulated connection that he makes between his friends' inability to reckon with his own recent brush with death and their further inability to make room in their moral universe for

the ambiguous actuality that in point of fact Duck Caldwell presents—it is some barely traceable relation that he
perceives between the two insensibilities that leads him,
day after day, to put off telling them about his meeting in
New York with Gifford Maxim. But, at last, he knows that
he mustn't postpone the recital any longer, that further
delay in apprising Nancy and Arthur of what they are
bound to feel an ominously momentous development will
seem to them inexplicable and a sort of personal betrayal.
So, on a certain evening, he steels himself and plunges in.
The Crooms are, of course, appalled by Maxim's bald
violation of all the decorums of radical politics, by his
having forsaken the heroic role to which they had elected
him: they declare him to be not merely mad but insane.
And they are not pleased with Laskell for having brought
such news.

Indeed, their confoundedness turns into something like
nausea and disgust when, a few days later, the morning's
mail brings the latest issue of *The New Era*, which carries
Maxim's name on the masthead and an article of his on
Melville's *Billy Budd* making evident that his recent pilgrimage has entailed not only a rejection of his former
Marxism but the embrace of a highly dialectical Christian
theology. The article—which bears the title "Spirit and
Law"—argues that Claggart represents the principle of Evil
and that Billy, though not wholly pure, is pure enough to
stand for Spirit in the world of Necessity, Necessity or
Law being represented by Captain Vere. Melville's parable,
Maxim maintains, is quite beyond the comprehension of
modern liberalism, "that loose body of middle class opinion which includes such ideas as progress, collectivism and
humanitarianism."[4] For, whereas "Vere must rule the

[4]Lionel Trilling, *E. M. Forster* (Norfolk, Conn.: New Directions,
1943), p. 13.

world of Necessity because Claggart—Evil—exists," modern
liberals suppose that "Spirit should find its complete expression at once" and that

> . . . Captain Vere is culpable because he does not acquit
> Billy in defiance of all Law. To them, Vere's suffering at
> being unable to do so is a mere sentimentality. It is even
> an hypocrisy.

But Melville's perception, says Maxim, is that, for as long
as there is Evil in the world, "Law must exist, and it—not
Spirit—must have the rule." And his essay goes on to speak
of Billy Budd's role in Melville's design as essentially Chris-
tological, of Vere's tragic choice being that of "God the
Father, who must condemn his own Son," though "not as
in the familiar transaction of . . . [orthodox] theology, as
a sacrifice and an atonement, but for the sake of the Son
himself, for the sake of Spirit in humanity"; and much is
said of tragedy and love and of their irrefragable mutual-
ity.

This reading of Melville's story, as well as the meditation
on the problem of evil for which it is the vehicle, does
indeed prove to be beyond the comprehension of these
enlightened people. The Crooms are simply disgusted by
what they take to be the reactionary obscurantism of
Maxim's new creed, and to Laskell it conveys nothing but
"the odor of corruption."

But, though it is the novel's purpose that Maxim shall
finally be bested, it intends that his routing shall be the
consequence of an agon to be arranged between him and
these friends whom he has so shocked by his apostasies.
And this occasion does in due course eventuate. Maxim
and Kermit Simpson, it seems, have quickly achieved an
easy relationship in their collaboration on Simpson's magazine, and they shortly appear together in the neighborhood, driving in with a gleaming new trailer in which they

are taking a brief trip through New England that they propose to interrupt for a few days of camping in the Crooms' district.

Their visit happens to coincide with the village's annual church bazaar—which is always arranged to culminate in an entertainment. And, for this year's performance, little Susan Caldwell is scheduled to present a recitation of the four stanzas prefixed to Blake's Jerusalem. She has been rehearsing her part for weeks, and Laskell, having won the child's affection, has sometimes been her audience. She has learned the poem in the old elocutionary manner recommended by her mother; and, as she declaims it one morning, Laskell advises against the gesture of passionate refusal she makes by stamping her foot at the line "I will *not* cease from Mental Fight." He suggests that the line ought to be read on a level: "*I will not cease. . . .*" He immediately regrets his interference, but Susan, being persuaded of the rightness of his advice, insists on altering her procedure. On the afternoon of the bazaar, however, when she comes to this line, she does it unthinkingly in the old way, with the stamp of the foot. Then so great is her dismay at the error that she is unable to go on until Laskell gently gives her a cue from his seat among the assembled guests. But her childish aplomb quickly returns: she does at last carry the thing off with a great flourish, and receives a loudly approving applause. Her drunken father, though, has entered the church during her recital, and, when she leaves the stage, he lurches forward, saying to the child: "A fine one you are. A disgrace." And, as the stunned little girl looks up into his face, he strikes her twice: she falls, and, when she is picked up, she is dead. Her heart has failed. (Emily had earlier disclosed to Laskell that she had never permitted Duck to learn of Susan's heart ailment, fearing that, were he to have knowledge of it, he, in his arrogantly robust physicality, would not "respect" his child.)

Now it is this desolating event that establishes the occasion for the agon between Maxim and his lowering friends. Laskell and the Crooms, and even Maxim and Kermit Simpson (who offers to defray the funeral expenses), are deeply touched by the searing grief that is felt by the entire community. After the funeral and the interment, the weather turns wet and cold, and they sit around the Crooms' fireplace, trying with painful difficulty to discover what it is that this sad moment requires in the way of definition and judgment. The Crooms do not hold Duck responsible, they rightly refuse to think of him as a murderer: he was, they say, "just the agent of fate." "It's not his fault," Nancy insists, and Arthur explains that "social causes, environment, education or lack of education, economic pressure, the character-pattern imposed by society, in this case a disorganized society, all go to . . . account for any given individual's actions." "Yes," says Nancy, "We can't say he's to blame personally, individually. But," she adds, "I can't stand the idea of having him around me. Not that I'd be afraid, but I'd always be thinking that this man killed his child." And this is Maxim's reply:

> "Nancy's dilemma is an inevitable one. She refuses to say that Caldwell has any responsibility, any blame or guilt. And then she refuses to allow him to come near her. . . . I reverse your whole process. I believe that Duck Caldwell—like you or me or any of us—is wholly responsible for his acts. . . . And for eternity. . . . That is what gives him value in my eyes—his eternal, everlasting responsibility. . . . And yet in my system there is one thing that yours lacks. In my system, although there is never-ending responsibility, there is such a thing as

mercy. . . . Duck can be forgiven. I can personally forgive him because I believe that God can forgive him. . . .
For you—no responsibility for the individual, but no
forgiveness. For me—ultimate, absolute responsibility
for the individual, but mercy. . . ."

It is at this juncture that the novel grants Laskell what it
expects us to consider his supreme moment of illumination. He says: "An absolute freedom from responsibility—that much of a child none of us can be. An absolute
responsibility—that much of a divine or metaphysical essence none of us is." And immediately the room is filled
with anger—because, as it is suggested, neither the Crooms
nor Maxim can tolerate "an idea in modulation," because
both, essentially, are already the creatures of some tyrannous absolutism of the far future. Nancy and Arthur
accuse Laskell of "name-calling" and "shilly-shally." Maxim, in what Laskell feels to be the first sneer he has ever
heard his friend permit himself, replies: "Neither beast nor
angel! You're not being original. Pascal said it long ago."
And, from this point on, it is Laskell and Maxim who are
at the center of the struggle. Maxim magnanimously concedes that Laskell is speaking up for "the human being in
maturity, at once responsible and conditioned," that
Laskell's testimony is made out of "the old knowledge
of . . . the human fate." "But," as he declares, "it's the *old*
knowledge": ". . . it won't last, John, it's diminishing now.
It is too late for that—the Renaissance is dead." Laskell,
however, is stubborn in his refusal to acquiesce: he wants
man to have his full human stature—neither beast nor
angel. Indeed, on the capital point at issue, there is for him
so much at stake that at last he forswears all dialectic,
declining to surrender his most fundamental faith to the
crucible of debate. That is to say, he rejects Maxim's
Christian position not because it is untrue but because it is

held by an ex-Communist. And the novel very clearly wants us to be persuaded of how right he is, in peremptorily dismissing Maxim as one who is simply riding the pendulum of the *Zeitgeist*—from one extreme idealism to another.

So to summarize the book is, of course, to betray what is one of the most absorbing and one of the most brilliantly written novels of our time. In an interview in 1955, as he reflected on the course taken by his career, Mr. Trilling recalled how, as the years had gone by, "one essay [had] led to another" and denied that he felt any great displeasure at having devoted his major efforts to criticism; but, as he spoke of a second novel on which he was then at work but which has never appeared, he admitted that he would perhaps be happier with a novelist's identity than with a critic's. And it may, indeed, be reckoned a very considerable loss to the literature of fiction that he has been so largely deflected from the novelist's vocation by his commitments (over more than forty years of residence on the English faculty at Columbia) to teaching and critical work. For in its probing of the lesions of selfhood that can be laid open in the people of our age by the Idea, *The Middle of the Journey* reveals a talent such as few American novelists have had for dramatizing the complex interrelationships in modern experience between thought (or ideology) and passion; and it asks at least to be measured in the terms we find appropriate to such books as Malraux's *Les Noyers de l'Altenbourg* and Camus' *La Peste* and Bellow's *Mr. Sammler's Planet.* It is, to be sure (as the late Morton Zabel remarked in his 1947 review), a novel whose "sequence of scenes and confrontations among characters [is] virtually syllogistic."[5] But in no way is it

[5]Morton Dauwen Zabel, "The Straight Way Lost," *The Nation,* 165, no. 16 (18 October 1947): 414.

flattened into any sort of merely pedagogic document by its dialectical purpose and structure; and, despite the stark economy of its anecdote, the tensions belonging to the particular human reality under examination are mounted with a kind of brilliant inevitability that we find wonderfully engrossing and whose effect upon us it seems right to speak of as being that of *cogency.*

Yet, for all the remarkable subtlety (of language and perception) with which the novel explores the bafflements by which the liberal intelligence was beset in the middle years of this century, it does suffer a certain failure of cogency in its choice of method for handling Gifford Maxim. For so committed is it to the centrist vision of the human fact—neither beast nor angel—and so resolved is it to uphold the secular legacy of the Enlightenment that, having admitted into its purview a man whose analysis of the world descends from Augustine and Pascal and Kierkegaard, it can find no way of dealing with him other than the "ideological" way of treating him as one who is simply bestride a pendulum of the *Zeitgeist.* The Crooms and John Laskell are outraged at having to face a friend who has deserted that system of faith with which they have wanted to keep the relation of cautious fellow-travelers. But they are far more outraged that one who formerly gave his suffrage to the great executive force of a political faith intending to impose community on an imperfect world should now have fought his way through to the belief, as he says, that "My community with men is that we are children of God." And that he should enunciate such a faith in the terms not of a primitivistic fundamentalism but of an immensely sophisticated dialectic simply compounds his offense. Nor can one escape the sense of their outrage being that which provides the principle of sentiment executively operative in the crucial closing scenes of the novel. For, despite its occasional feats of

self-transcendence—in managing to acknowledge Maxim as
the humanly formidable man he is—the novel does finally
insist on bullying its antagonist into the position of being
merely a clever specialist in sharp practice. Unpleasant
motives are imputed to him but not *proven* (as, by way of
what is dramatically *shown*, a work of fiction proves its
case)—and he is simply *declared* to be an opportunist who
has found one system of idealism to have lost its power,
who discerns that the time is "ripe for a competing system," and who (clever homiletician that he is) is now
busily preparing an arsenal of defense for his new creed. So
in such a man, it is suggested, one can only be repelled by
"the odor of corruption."

It is surely a little astonishing that, given all the sophisti-
cations at work in the novel, it does manage so cruelly to
take advantage of one of its major personages. (And, for
this, it can find no exculpation in the phenomenon that
occasionally figured in the post-war American time out of
which it comes, of a former Communist being graduated
from the catechumenical chambers of a prominent ecclesi-
astic.) But, of course, an authorial intelligence always
defines itself not alone in terms of its capacity freely to
order the material with which it deals but also in terms of
those particular partialities of perspective by which its
freedom is in certain respects significantly qualified. And
the treatment accorded Gifford Maxim in *The Middle of
the Journey* is but the measure of Mr. Trilling's own
partiality, as it is also the measure of his ambivalence of
feeling with respect to Arthur and Nancy Croom. For,
though he wants to press a very serious charge against the
constituency of that modern liberal intelligentsia which
the Crooms represent—for the too frequent inadequacy of
imagination with which they approach the moral life—his
own most fundamental position remains one of commitment to the great traditions of secular, liberal humanism

by which people like the Crooms are ultimately sustained. It is, moreover, a commitment held so tenaciously, so resolutely, that any account of the world that seems to envisage a dimension of Transcendence must, however severely, be swept aside as promising only a betrayal of the "idea in modulation"—the idea, that is, of man as neither beast nor angel but as the occupant of the middle region where Nature and Spirit reach that point of intersection studied by Cicero and Marcus Aurelius, by Montaigne and Rousseau, by John Stuart Mill and Matthew Arnold, by Hegel and Freud. And the mind controlling *The Middle of the Journey* is not prepared to brook any theological possibility precisely because what it wants to be the burden of its own main affirmation is nothing other than the humanist and intractably secular testimony—to the "modulated" reality of man in his full human autonomy, at once responsible and conditioned, neither beast nor angel.

Now one feels impelled to speak of the affirmation Mr. Trilling has most essentially wanted to make as having entailed a certain burden, because, as his thought has proceeded over the past twenty-five years, principally through his criticism, his sense of cultural reality has constantly enforced upon him a recognition of the threatened status of that "modulated" vision descending from those who have managed (in the manner, say, of Wordsworth and Keats, or of the Marx of the *Economic and Philosophical Manuscripts* and of Freud) to be responsive at once to the Enlightenment and to Romanticism. And it is, indeed, in the synthesis of the Enlightenment's endorsement of the life of reason, of man's assuming full responsibility for his condition in history, with the insistence of Romanticism that there is more in our human *Lebenswelt* than reason can precisely measure and codify—it is in the nice amalgamation of these two accents that Mr. Trilling finds a true adumbration of a complete secular wisdom about the human situation. It was not wholly accidental, we suspect, that, after completing his Columbia doctoral dissertation on Arnold, the first major job he turned his hand to was a little book on E. M. Forster, for here, in the author of *Howards End* and *A Passage to India* (as he was at pains to remind us), was a thoroughly secular man whose whole imaginative effort was calculated, in effect, to say to us "Only connect . . ."—only connect reason and imagination, the head and the heart: and do not oversimplify. But, almost everywhere, as it seems to Mr. Trilling, the full secular wisdom about man has been by way of being attenuated in the last hundred years, and not most seriously by those of Gifford Maxim's party who cast their vote for some norm of Transcendence but rather by those (of the party of Arthur and Nancy Croom) who, intending to support the fully modulated ideal of secular autonomy, do nevertheless betray that standard in their submission to some irresistible penchant for oversimplification.

Thus it comes to be that the phrase making the title of his book of 1950, the book that guaranteed his American reputation—*The Liberal Imagination*—is very nearly a pejorative in the lexicon of this most steadfast votary of the liberal tradition. For, though its interests are closest to his heart, the "liberal imagination," in its recurrent failure to reckon with the "variousness and possibility," with the "complexity and difficulty" of the human enterprise, has too often not been good enough. So the great effort undertaken in the essays comprising the book of 1950 was not that of "confirming liberalism in its sense of general rightness but rather [of] . . . putting under some degree of pressure" certain of its characteristic weaknesses and failings. And it was the book on Forster that made evident the kind of touchstone on which Mr. Trilling relied, since, there, the decisive consideration that establishes Forster's very great distinction is that, though writing out of a thoroughly secular outlook, he is yet "clearly in the romantic line" in his openness to the irreducible complexity and mystery contained within the human universe. It is this *wholeness* of vision (embracing both the prose and the passion of life, responsive at once to the naturalist perspectives of the Enlightenment and the expansively humanistic perspectives of Romanticism) that regularly keeps him, in Mr. Trilling's analysis, from practicing any sort of reductionism on the manifold economy of the fully human. Forster knows that such order as may be found in the world of human affairs rests upon no simple logic, that good is never simply good and bad is never simply bad, that the immediate actualities of our lives are always an affair of good-and-evil. And, as a consequence, he is protected against that surprise by which modern liberalism is recurrently overtaken when confronted by the contradictions and paradoxes of the moral life, a surprise which is then often followed by disillusionment and fatigue. Indeed, it is the sober worldliness of Forster's "moral realism"—in which there is nothing of quietism or of indifference to the urgencies of history—that saves him from any eschatological impatience with the finitude of man: his "naturalism is positive and passionate," but it does not carry within itself any discontent with the nature of human nature. He knows that we do not guarantee a brighter future by rejecting the past; that authority and society are not, in and of themselves, stupid and disposable inconveniences; that the practical cannot be attained through the impractical. In him, there is nothing of that "taste for the unconditioned ... that is always being fooled by the world. ..." He presents, in short, an example of a liberalism resourceful and competent because it does not affirm its confidence in reason by making reason something mechanical and devoid of imagination. So Mr. Trilling's argument proceeds; and, in its relation to the

matter at hand, the case is made with a brilliant persuasive-
ness, however much we may jib at a ranking of Forster's
work that offers the paramount garland to *Howards End*
rather than to *A Passage to India.* But, in the context of
Mr. Trilling's own thought, what is of primary importance
is the directness with which the book on Forster sets forth
the normative principles under which he has proposed to
institute an evaluation of modern literary and intellectual
life.

In the years of the 1940s, however, when he was writing
the essays that were eventually to form *The Liberal Imagination,* his strongest impression of the climate of liberal
thought was of how notably deficient it was in that sobri-
ety and sanity that made Forster's special distinction. It
was not, of course, a very numerous society—the people,
that is, who read *The Nation* and *Partisan Review,* who
lived politically on the radical fringes of the Democratic
Party, who held enlightened views on Negroes and Jews,
who kept "a ready if mild suspiciousness of the profit
motive, a belief in progress, science, social legislation,
planning, and international cooperation, perhaps especially
where Russia is in question." But, though not numerous,
in a period "when Mind—conscious, verbalized mind—[had
become] ... an important element"[6] in the politics of
culture and when Ideas had become Weapons (as it was
said at the time in the title of a popular book by the
historian and journalist, Max Lerner), the educated class,
for all its seeming marginality with respect to the centers
of social and political dominion, was by no means itself
without a certain crucial power. And what chiefly dis-
tressed Mr. Trilling was that, at the very moment when
liberal thought should begin to count for so much, it
should prove to be so unstable an affair—with its eagerness

[6]Trilling, *E. M. Forster*, p. 122.

"to elect a way of life which shall be satisfactory once and for all, time without end"; its "coldness to historical thought"; and its secret hope "that man's life in politics, which is to say, man's life in history, shall come to an end." So, remembering John Stuart Mill's suggestion (in his essay on Coleridge), that the prayer of every thoughtful adherent of liberalism ought to be " 'Lord, enlighten thou our enemies. . . .' " but being also mindful of how impossible it is to devise an opposition which shall devote itself to keeping us clearheaded and cogent, Mr. Trilling appointed himself in the 1940s to the not inconsiderable task of undertaking from within the liberal camp to put under a "degree of pressure" some of its most widely prevalent habits of thought and imagination.

Again, what he would seem to have felt to be the chief cause of the crisis in liberalism was its failure to keep its legacy from the Enlightenment informed by the sensibilities of Romanticism: so devoted has it been to the life of reason, and so committed to its vision of the world as in every way susceptible of rational direction, that "it drifts toward a denial of the emotions and the imagination." The intention to achieve a rational organization of life promotes the tendency to view the world as wholly comprised of that which is rationally manipulable. A special authority is accorded those "theories and principles, particularly in relation to the nature of the human mind, that justify" such a conception of reality. And the result is, of course, the further tendency to oversimplify. For, however admirable in certain respects may be the intention to organize the world in a rational way,

> . . . organization means delegation, and agencies, and bureaus, and technicians, and . . . the ideas that can survive delegation, that can be passed on to agencies and bureaus and technicians, incline to be ideas of a certain

kind and of a certain simplicity: they give up something of their largeness and modulation and complexity in order to survive. The lively sense of contingency and possibility, and of those exceptions to the rule which may be the beginning of the end of the rule—this sense does not suit well with the impulse to organization.

In short, a besetting tendency of the modern, secular, liberal mind is to deal impatiently with whatever seems inclined to elude the nets of systematic formulation. Intelligence is conceived to be the power of reckoning with fact, with material fact—which is always imagined as "hard, resistant, unformed, impenetrable, and [even] unpleasant. And that mind is alone felt to be trustworthy which most resembles this reality by most nearly reproducing the sensations it affords." The distinguishing feature of the real is thought to be its externality, its coarse, "bedrock, concrete quality"; and it is supposed that reality stands only to be betrayed by "subjectivity," by the internal, by complication and modulation and irony: these, it is held, can never get us through gross dangers and difficulties. So it is, Mr. Trilling maintains, that "the residuary legatees of the Enlightenment" are often by way of converting the liberal faith "into the very opposite of its avowed intention of liberation."

A primary exhibit brought forward in *The Liberal Imagination* of what is restrictively positivistic in the tendency of liberal doctrine is the case of Vernon Parrington, whose *Main Currents in American Thought* was over a long period perhaps the most influential account of our national literature—until it became the subject of Lionel Trilling's devastating appraisal. And what chiefly interests Mr. Trilling in Parrington is the classic way in which *Main Currents* formulates "the suppositions about our culture which are held by the American middle class so far as that class is at

all liberal in its social thought and so far as it begins to
understand that literature has anything to do with society." Indeed, for him Parrington stands as the great diarist
of the liberal imagination, because he expresses with extremest candor its chronic uneasiness before all evidences
of style and thought in literature and art, its chronic
"belief that there exists an opposition between reality and
mind and that one must enlist oneself in the party of
reality." Parrington considers Hawthorne's researches into
what he calls "the hidden, furtive recesses of the soul" to
be irrelevant to a democratic culture: Hawthorne, he says,
was "forever dealing with shadows." So, too, were Melville
and Henry James. And since "shadows" do not themselves
have, for Parrington, any status in the world of the real, he
dismisses the authors of *Moby Dick* and *The Portrait of a
Lady* as "escapist": the creatures of their imagination are
only projections of "brooding fancy, externalizations of
hypothetical subtleties"—as is also the case with those of
Poe (overborne by "the atrabilious wretchedness of a dip-
somaniac") and Edith Wharton and Scott Fitzgerald (a
"candle . . . burnt out"). And Parrington's enthusiasms are
reserved for William Cullen Bryant and Whitman, for the
Mark Twain of *Huckleberry Finn,* and for such writers as
Hamlin Garland and Jack London and Ole Rölvaag and
"the incomparable" James Branch Cabell.

But, as Mr. Trilling insists, despite his occasional great,
shocking lapses of taste, Parrington's taste was not generally something terribly bad; and his failures in aesthetic
judgment are, therefore, most basically to be ascribed not
so much to defective taste as to "his assumptions about
the nature of reality"—as something "sobersided, even
grim," and untransmissible through the human imagination. In this, however—in his "belief in the incompatibility
of mind and reality"—Parrington was by no means alone:
indeed, though he died in 1929, he still in the early 1940s

stood as the great exemplar of what Mr. Trilling at the
time was calling "the literary academicism of liberalism"—
a body of opinion in the colleges and universities whose
"doctrinaire indulgence . . . toward Theodore Dreiser" and
Sherwood Anderson was counterbalanced by the careful-
ness of its acerbity toward Henry James. As Mr. Trilling
noticed at the time, it was the habit of liberal intellectuals
to acknowledge the depth of James's tragic sense and the
subtlety of his moral perceptiveness, but then to submit
him "to the ultimate question: of what use, of what actual
political use, are his gifts . . . of what possible practical
value in our world of impending disaster can James's work
be?" Whereas Dreiser's ideas—his "dim, awkward specula-
tion . . . his lust for . . . 'Life itself' "—were regularly exempted from any close bargaining, his lack of wit and his
crude provincialism and his intellectual vulgarity being
taken as simply an expression of "the sad, lovable, honor-
able faults of reality itself." And, as Mr. Trilling considered
the imparity of the verdict accorded James and Dreiser by
liberal criticism, the accent of his speech grew angry and
indignant:

> We live, understandably enough, with the sense of ur-
> gency; our clock, like Baudelaire's, has had the hands
> removed and bears the legend, "It is later than you
> think." But with us it is always a little too late for mind,
> yet never too late for honest stupidity; always a little
> too late for understanding, never too late for righteous,
> bewildered wrath; always too late for thought, never too
> late for naive moralizing. We seem to like to condemn
> our finest but not our worst qualities by pitting them
> against the exigency of time.

Nor did he turn in *The Liberal Imagination* exclusively
to the issues of literary life for examples of the myopia to
which the liberal mind is subject. For the huge commotion

that had been created by the appearance in 1948 of the Kinsey Report,[7] as it came to be called, made an episode in which Mr. Trilling found a large symptomatic significance, at once in the effort being made by the American public at self-enlightenment through social statistics and, more particularly even, in the assumptions on which the Report itself rested. He took the great *éclat* provoked by the Report to signalize the belief not just of physicians and biologists and social workers but of the educated class at large that a behavioristic science was now the agency of our cultural imagination best equipped to deal authoritatively with questions of sexual conduct, and this seemed to represent one very important symptom of our new spirituality. But then, apart from the general eagerness of the educated class to sponsor a lively commerce between sex and science, there was the Report itself, in its own massive accumulation of charts and tables; and what chiefly interested Mr. Trilling in the document was not the elaborateness with which its graphs and tables publicized "an almost universal involvement in the sexual life and therefore much variety of conduct." For this, as he said, "was taken for granted in any comedy that Aristophanes put on the stage." No, it was not the anecdotal aspect of the Report that he found significant but rather its assumptive aspect— by which, as he supposed, it was as much commended to the American public as by its elaborate anecdote (involving such personae as the "scholarly and skilled lawyer" with an orgasmic frequency of thirty times a week over a period of thirty years). And it is, therefore, to an analysis of the Report's basic assumptions that one of the most brilliant essays in *The Liberal Imagination* is devoted.

Given its heavy bias toward quantitative methods, the

[7]See Alfred C. Kinsey, Wardell B. Pomeroy, and Clyde E. Martin, *Sexual Behavior in the Human Male* (Philadelphia: Saunders, 1948).

Report wants, of course, to separate the sexual life from the total psychic structure, as if the whole actuality of sex were anatomical and physiological; and thus Mr. Trilling is at pains to remark its "extravagant fear of all ideas that do not seem to be . . . immediately dictated by simple physical fact," its awkwardness in handling ideas involving "a specifically human situation"—as, for example, in its view of male potency. The Report resists the folk feeling, that the male's potency is to be measured by his ability to postpone his own orgasm until the woman has been brought to climax: indeed, it even defends the male who ejaculates immediately upon intromission, saying that "it would be difficult to find another situation in which an individual who was quick and intense in his responses was labeled anything but superior. . . ." To which Mr. Trilling replies that "by such reasoning the human male who is quick and intense in his leap to the lifeboat is natural and superior, however inconvenient . . . his speed and intensity may be to the wife he leaves standing on the deck, as is also the man . . . who bites his dentist's fingers, who kicks the child who annoys him, who bolts his—or another's—food, who is incontinent of his feces." It is with a similar sharpness of wit that he exposes much else in the Report's impertinence and crudity—its great penchant for the argument *de animalibus*, its assumption that orgasmic frequency must be the sign of a robust sexuality, that common practice establishes the only relevant standard for judging sexual behavior (that it is, in other words, not to be judged at all). Indeed, the Report's way of fostering "a democratic pluralism of sexuality" does, finally, present itself to Mr. Trilling as a major instance of that aversion from complexity and modulation which constitutes a basic weakness of the liberal mind. For the Report wants to sponsor a broad ratification of variety in the forms of sexuality; but it assumes that this generous goal is to be

realized simply by the *acceptance* of whatever it is that
men actually do, by the acceptance "not merely in the
scientific sense but also in the social sense, in the sense,
that is, that no judgment must be passed on [it], that any
conclusion drawn from [it] which perceives values and
consequences will turn out to be 'undemocratic.' " Thus it
was that the entire event comprised by the Report itself
and its dramatic reception at the end of the forties did at
last strike Mr. Trilling as only another expression of that
unfortunate tendency to oversimplify often represented by
the liberal thought of the period.

It is, one feels, just his impatience with a mentality itself
so often impatient of the multitudinous distinctions contained by human experience that has prompted Mr. Trilling over many years to keep so vivid a sense of the
greatness of Freud, on whom he has written on several
occasions with immense distinction (in *The Liberal Imagination*, in *Beyond Culture*, and in his most recent book
*Sincerity and Authenticity*). For this Viennese Jew who so
greatly extended the frontiers of man's self-knowledge is
without any impulse to "narrow and simplify the human
world": instead, he wants always to "open and complicate
it." Mr. Trilling knows, of course, how erroneous is Thomas Mann's portrait of Freud as a poet of the "night side" of
life: he knows that Freud's "Apollonian" side was by no
means secondary and accidental, that he was in many ways
deeply committed to that late nineteenth-century European ethos which conceived a positivistic rationalism to be
"the very form and pattern of intellectual virtue." Yet he
regards the Freudian man as

> a creature of far more dignity and far more interest than
> the man which any other modern system has been able
> to conceive. Despite popular belief to the contrary,
> man, as Freud conceives him, is not to be understood by

any simple formula (such as sex) but is rather an in-extricable tangle of culture and biology. And not being simple, he is not simply good; he has, as Freud says somewhere, a kind of hell within him from which arise everlastingly the impulses which threaten his civiliza-tion. He has the faculty of imagining for himself more in the way of pleasure and satisfaction than he can pos-sibly achieve. . . . His best qualities are the result of a struggle whose outcome is tragic. Yet he is a creature of love. . . .

And the great dignity and charm of the Freudian vision for Mr. Trilling consist not only in the profundity of its psychological analysis but also in the fact that its ultimate "desire for man is only that he should be human"—neither beast nor angel.

Now it is doubtless his own great desire to "open and complicate" the liberal imagination that has led Mr. Trill-ing in his more purely literary work to make the point of intersection between literature and society the focus of his criticism. Given his own semantic, of course, he would doubtless himself prefer to have that extramural dimension to which his criticism has related the literary imagination specified as "politics." And, to be sure, he is constantly to be found meditating upon the coalescence in modern cul-ture of these two spaces, of the literary space and of that which he speaks of as politics. But the more closely Mr. Trilling's essays are examined the more evanescent be-comes that region of meaning with which the term politics permits itself in his usage to be identified, and it does finally seem that the speciality with which the term be-haves in his writing is to be understood only when it is connected with that particular moment in his criticism when he quite explicitly speaks of evanescence. It is in the essay in *The Liberal Imagination* entitled "Manners, Morals, and the Novel" that he speaks of his interest in that "whole evanescent context" which surrounds "all the explicit statements that a people makes through its art, religion, architecture, legislation," the "dim mental region of intention" which constitutes "that part of a culture . . . made up of half-uttered or unuttered or unutterable expressions of value"—where "assumption rules." Here it is, on this deepest level of a people's life, that we hear the "hum and buzz" of that "multifarious intention" which is the real seat of complexity in any elaborately organized society. Inevitably, as Mr. Trilling supposes, literature supervenes upon and enters into this intricate, shadowy province of a culture, because it is just at this depth that the great ideas of a people—about birth and death, about fate and freedom—have their most potent life. And when he speaks (in the essay on "The Function of the Little Magazine" in *The Liberal Imagination*) of our present "fate, for better or worse, [as] . . . political," when he speaks of the deep places of the modern imagination as a region of "politics"—which is, I think, what the term does in fact designate in his thought—his actual meaning is that, in a secular culture having the degree of complexity that ours has, the deep places of the spirit are, indeed, "politicized," in the sense that, there, a great legion of divergent ideas *compete* with one another for our assent and loyalty. As he says ("Art and Fortune," *The Liberal Imagination*),

> Nowadays everyone is involved in ideas—or, to be more accurate, in ideology. . . . Every person we meet in the course of our daily life, no matter how unlettered he may be, is groping with sentences toward a sense of his life and his position in it; and he has what almost always goes with an impulse to ideology, a good deal of animus and anger. What would so much have pleased the social

philosophers of an earlier time has come to pass—
ideological organization has cut across class organization, generating loyalites and animosities which are perhaps even more intense than those of class.

So, unavoidably, the great human reality with which literature in the modern period has had to deal has been that of
"politics"—namely, the kinds of tensions, the kind of
drama, engendered in a pluralist society by ideas, most
especially when they are "living things, inescapably connected with our wills and desires." And in this sense, then,
it may, indeed, be that we should speak of politics rather
than society as that whose relation to literature Mr. Trilling has made the focus of his criticism. For his central
subject of inquiry has been that complex reciprocity of
pressure between literature and the Idea which is a primary
fact of the modern scene.

In the essays comprising *The Liberal Imagination,* the
particular body of ideas (or ideology) whose relation to
modern literature fell under Mr. Trilling's scrutiny represented that great modern passion for the clear and distinct
idea which, in its intolerance of variousness and contrariety, inevitably sponsors those schemes of thought calculated to diminish or attentuate the human reality. Perhaps
the most immediate *mystique* he was resisting was that
which had been established by the pieties of the American
intelligentsia of the Left in the period of the nineteen-
thirties and early forties, when the utopianism of the
Communist Party and its fellow-travelers was a dominant
spiritual force. But the oversimplification of the present in
the interests of "the far future" was for him but a type
and example of that larger malaise of liberal thought which
involved such an infatuation with rationality as inclined
the modern intelligence to expel from the circle of its
attention whatever resisted easy rational mastery. So,

whether he was talking about the *Annals* of Tacitus or Henry James's *The Princess Casamassima*, about Parrington's *Main Currents* or the Kinsey Report, about Kipling or Freud or Scott Fitzgerald, he was wanting to hold up models either of a tonic kind of "realism" or of some typical stupidity of liberal progressivism. It was a similar purpose at work in the more purely speculative pieces in the book of 1950—in the famous essays on "Manners, Morals, and the Novel," on "Art and Fortune," and on "The Meaning of a Literary Idea." And the collection as a whole constituted what needs hardly now to be remarked, as we stand at a remove from it of more than twenty years—namely, one of the most brilliant bodies of testimony in the whole literature of modern literary criticism and one of the great American books of this century.

*       *       *

The assessment of the liberal imagination which Mr. Trilling had begun in the 1940s was carried forward into a new phase by the essays making up his book of 1955, *The Opposing Self*. Here, as it now seems, his primary theme was shifting somewhat, from his earlier concern with the oversimplifications of reality sponsored by the liberal intelligence to a new preoccupation with that penchant for life in the angelic mode which is fostered by the passion for the clear and distinct idea. Mr. Trilling does not himself at any point have recourse to the category of "angelism," but it is a formulation which, in its employment by Jacques Maritain (in his book on Descartes[8]), exactly renders his sense of what is frequently problematic in that conception of the self's relation to the world which has been deeply a

[8]See Jacques Maritain, *The Dream of Descartes*, trans. Mabelle L. Andison (New York: Philosophical Library, 1944).

part of the ethos of secular, liberal thought since the Enlightenment. The angel, presumably, is a creature whose creatureliness does not require it to submit to or be ruled by any of the exigencies of nature and history: it is angelic just because, despite its creatureliness, it lives outside those exigencies, in a realm of pure spirit where, being unafflicted by any of the limitations of sense, it has immediate access to the realm of the essences. Now by "angelism" Maritain means that type of modern mentality which considers the high abstraction, the clear and distinct idea, to be the great thing deserving pursuit, rather than the concrete object. And it is for him a mentality which proves itself to be angelic by so exalting reason in its Cartesian vacuum as in effect to withdraw from any commitment to the contingent and bounded world of the human creature. Which is precisely what *The Opposing Self* finds to be a characteristic stance of the modern sensibility.

It is the great opening essay on Keats in the book of 1955 which, again, reveals most immediately Mr. Trilling's touchstone. The essay is filled with admiration and tribute, not only by reason of Keats's astounding lordship of language but also because his prodigious literary gift was so constantly guided by an intention at once to affirm "the creativity of the self that opposes circumstance" and to acknowledge, despite "his partisanship with social amelioration," the unlikelihood of life being ever "ordered in such a way that its condition might be anything but tragic." He affirms the creativity of "the self that is imagination and desire, that, like Adam, assigns names and values to things, and that can realize what it envisions." But, at the same time, he never supposes that life in the heroic mode is a *simple* possibility; he "never deceives himself into believing that the power of the imagination is sovereign, that it can make the power of circumstance of no account." He knows that man is not a beast, and he knows that neither is he an angel. And it is the steadiness (both in his letters and in the poetry) with which these "two knowledges"—that life deserves to be called blessed and that its circumstances are nevertheless often cursed—it is the steadiness with which the "two knowledges" are held in integral relationship that constitutes for Mr. Trilling the great sanity of Keats's genius, the thing that makes him a great "image of health" in modern literature. The thoroughgoing secularity of Keats's general outlook leads Mr. Trilling to speak of it as having entailed a very "intense naturalism"; and a positive, confident naturalism does, of course, solicit his approbation. But what is most engaging in Keats is that his is a naturalism which never lost its firm grip on the essential fact, that it is the destiny of the self always to confront the difficult and limiting actualities of circumstance.

Indeed, for Mr. Trilling Keats stands not only as a great image of health but even as perhaps "the last image of health at the very moment when the sickness of Europe began to be apparent." For, as the essays in *The Opposing Self* make evident, what he sees as continually tempting in modern literary and intellectual life is the inclination to demand that life be pure spirit, the tendency to conceive the ideal posture of the self in relation to "the conditioned" as one of an "opposition" so radical as to entail an essentially angelic aspiration. "The dislike of the conditioned is in part what makes so many of us dissatisfied with our class situation, and guilty about it, and unwilling to believe that it has any reality, or that what reality it may have is a possible basis of moral or spiritual prestige, the moral or spiritual prestige which is the most valuable thing in the world to those of us who think a little. By extension, we are very little satisfied with the idea of family life—for us it is part of the inadequate bourgeois reality. Not that we don't live good-naturedly enough with our families, but when we do, we know that we are 'family men,' by definition cut off from the true realities of the spirit." Our great dream is of spirit unhedged about by the material circumstances of historical existence, by "the . . . conditions which the actual and the trivial make for it." So we are disenchanted with politics, weary of all the expediency and compromise it inevitably involves. For we want "the hot, direct relationship with godhead, or with the sources of life," and we cherish, therefore, the hidden and the ambiguous—most especially when they present themselves in the form of some great extreme idea (of alienation or madness or "historical necessity") which bristles with the eschatological urgency of our plight. In our literary preferences, we yield most readily to those writers who "enlarge all experience, [who] . . . involve it as soon as possible in history, myth, and the oneness of spirit." We expect our literature to deal with the singular and the eccentric; if it treats of human experience under the aspect of the common routine, it can win our approval only by rendering "the commonplace as it verges upon and becomes the rare and strange," since our metaphysical prejudices "lead us to feel the deficiency of what we call literal reality and to prefer what we call essential reality." We take it for granted that, in the handling of "essential reality," the tigers of wrath are wiser than the horses of instruction, for they are the great specialists in "the apocalyptic subject and the charismatic style," the great custodians of those dark and dubious places of the world that we inhabit. And Mr. Trilling's "we"—which has sometimes been felt to be troublesome—makes reference to no other class than the secular community of the contemporary liberal intelligentsia.

He knows, of course, that these attitudes, in so far as they have actual power in cultural life of the present time, may not be simply "legislated or criticized out of existence." But he does want to insist that, while they endure, certain of the great modes of the literary imagination will be accorded only a very listless and incommensurate regard, and precisely those which, were they to be fully confronted, might to some extent correct the imbalance represented by the angelic mind. So, in talking not only about Keats but also about Wordsworth and Orwell, about James and Howells, about the Dickens of *Little Dorrit* and the Jane Austen of *Mansfield Park*, about the Flaubert of *Bouvard and Pécuchet* and the Tolstoi of *Anna Karenina,* Mr. Trilling's intention is to hold up a group of modern writers exhibiting, to be sure, some diversity of viewpoint and (in their claims upon us) of distinction but nevertheless expressing—each in his own way—a vision of the autonomy of the self which is deeply informed by a kind of exemplary concern for the particularity and circumstantiality of man's life in the world.

If Keats has something like an heroic status in Mr. Trilling's design, it does not, however, surpass that which is granted Wordsworth. For it is the poet of the *Lyrical Ballads* and *The Prelude* who is for him one of the great examples of man's finding abundance of life "not . . . [in] militancy of spirit but . . . [in] calm submission to the law of things." "Much as he loved to affirm the dizzy raptures of sentience, of the ear and the eye and the mind, he also loved to move down the scale of being, to say that when the sentient spirit was sealed by slumber, when it was without motion and force, when it was like a rock or a stone or a tree, not hearing or seeing, and passive in the cosmic motion—that even then . . . existence was blessed." Indeed, Mr. Trilling considers it to have been a part of Wordsworth's genius that, as a poet, he should so constantly have kept alive his faculty for realizing in himself and awakening in us what he speaks of in the Second Book of *The Prelude* as "the sentiment of Being," the sense of life

being justified (as Mr. Trilling says) "in its elemental biological simplicity." But in our own period, when the reigning ontological vision is predominantly a vision of "the
dull not-being of life" or "the intense not-being of death,"
such an art as Wordsworth's—which looks the world in the
face and takes it for what it is[9]—will be felt to entail a
most objectionable element of quietism, since it does not
encourage us to deal with the world by condemning it or
withdrawing from it. *We* distrust "the sentiment of
Being": it seems to involve a negation of selfhood, of that
"ultimate and absolute power which the unconditioned
idea can develop." Yet it is Mr. Trilling's contention that,
for all of the modern reader's impatience with the accept-
ing attitudes towards the material and conditioned circumstances in which spirit must have its residence, these are,
nevertheless, attitudes with which the grain of literature
has often been most deeply inwrought. And it is of this
that he wants to present certain focal instances, in his
essays on such texts as *Bouvard and Pécuchet* and *Anna
Karenina,* as *Mansfield Park* and *Little Dorrit* and *The
Bostonians.*

Now it is the doctrine being put forward in *The Opposing Self* which was increasingly to challenge Mr. Trilling's
expository gift in the decade coming after the appearance
of that book. It was immediately followed in 1956 by a
brief collection of short pieces—*A Gathering of Fugitives*—
whose relaxed informality had been occasioned by the
special auspices under which most of them were originally
written: namely, the house organ of a book club ("The
Readers' Subscription") on whose selection panel he, along
with Jacques Barzun and W. H. Auden, served from 1951
until 1958. And even here, in his casual but brilliantly

[9]This phrase is lifted from a passage in Henry James's *The Princess
Casamassima* (spoken by Basil Ransom).

composed notes turned out (on such figures as E. M. Forster and Robert Graves, Henry Adams and Edmund Wilson, Freud and Santayana) for the club's patrons, his strongest preoccupations of the time are readily discernible—as when, for example, in discussing the sociologist David Riesman and his book *The Lonely Crowd,* he congratulates him for having "the intrusive curiosity" of a novelist about "the impingement of things upon spirit and of spirit upon things." Mr. Riesman, we are told, has a lively sense of the autonomy of the self; but he also knows what it is by which that autonomy is qualified, and he is an "artist of the conditioned."

It is, however, the volume which appeared in 1965—*Beyond Culture*—that presents, in its assemblage of the major essays that had appeared since *The Opposing Self,* the largest evidence of Mr. Trilling's continuing engrossment by the ideas that had centrally figured in the book of ten years before. As in each of the previous anthologies of his criticism, one's attention is most especially fixed in this volume by certain pivotal statements, amongst which it is the beautifully nuanced and spacious essay on "The Fate of Pleasure" that makes the readiest connection between the book as a whole and the work that had been exhibited a decade earlier in *The Opposing Self.* Here, it is Wordsworth who again offers an initial point of reference, particularly the bold declaration in his Preface to the *Lyrical Ballads* that it is "the grand elementary principle of pleasure" which consititutes "the naked and native dignity of man," that it is this principle by which man "knows, and feels, and lives, and moves." It is not the considerable intrinsic interest of Wordsworth's statement, however, that Mr. Trilling most wants to contemplate, but, rather, it is the quickened awareness of our present sense of life that the statement conveys, by the very greatness of the remove at which it stands from the secularized spirituality of our own period. For nothing, he suggests, is in poorer repute today than the notion that pleasure "in its primitive or radical aspect" belongs to the *native* and *naked* dignity of man and deserves, therefore, to be accorded a place of primacy in the life of the self. And he takes Dostoievski's *Notes from Underground* to be a text a part of whose role in the cultural life of our time has been that of providing an immensely prestigious sanction for the modern "repudiation of pleasure in favor of the gratification which may be found in unpleasure." That failed and bilious little clerk who is the protagonist of Dostoievski's great *novella* is sometimes thought to be a man whose *ressentiment* is occasioned by his envy, and his bitterness toward all those less disadvantaged than himself is conceived to be his way of making his own plight just barely tolerable—by turning his savage contempt on the purposefulness of life and the happiness which he has not managed to win. But this, as Mr. Trilling contends,

> . . . is only a small part of the truth. It is also true that he does not have because he does not wish to have; he has arranged his own misery—arranged it in the interests of his dignity, which is to say, of his freedom. For to want what is commonly thought to be appropriate to men, to want whatever it is, high or low, that is believed to yield pleasure, to be active about securing it, to use common sense and prudence to the end of gaining it, this is to admit and consent to the *conditioned* nature of man.

Now it is, one assumes, in the line of descent to be traced from Dostoievski's Underground Man that Mr. Trilling would place such representative literary personages of this century as Faulkner's Joe Christmas, Sartre's Antoine Roquentin, Graham Greene's Pinky, Beckett's Malone, William Burroughs' junkies, and many another, for all these (as Robert Musil's Ulrich says of himself) "will only cook with salt." And Mr. Trilling would say that this refusal to employ the sweeter condiments represents an aspiration towards a type of distinctively modern spirituality: this disavowal of "what is commonly thought to be appropriate to men" expresses an intention to reach for an independence and a dignity of spirit that shall be "beyond culture," beyond all the standards and predilections that are enforced upon us in our time by "the wonderful and terrible art of advertising." Indeed, he takes the modern devaluation of pleasure, particularly as it has found utterance in literature of the past hundred years, to be a sign of that "standing quarrel" with the official polity to which much of the finest energy of the liberal intelligence has been devoted. "Dostoievski's clerk has had his way with us," so much so that the *mystique* of unpleasure would seem to be very nearly unavailable to any sort of ironical scrutiny, since the only alternative to it appears to be some idiot doctrine of "positive thinking."

Nor is Mr. Trilling without a considerable sympathy for the motive he takes to be most deeply operative in the antihedonism distinguishing the advanced moral and aesthetic culture of the modern period. He does himself, indeed, want to record his opposition to all those modes of life and thought that would in effect convert human existence into a mere epiphenomenon of social-political process, or of the public economy, or of History. The specter of a world in which the human individual is without escape from the principalities and powers of his culture and is therefore infinitely malleable by them—this is for Mr. Trilling, one feels, the very definition of Hell. The fine essay, for example, on Freud in his book of 1965 clearly indicates how much his great devotion to the founder of psychoanalysis is in part elicited by the decisiveness with which Freud's system undertakes to "establish the self beyond the reach of culture." Freud's view of the self in its relation to culture does, of course, involve a tragic perspective. He knows that the individual is deeply formed by the highly complected matrix of personal and congregational relationships in which his life is set, but he knows that the inherent dynamism of the self impels it, in its search for fulfillment, to drive beyond the particular setting into which it is born, even to regard that context of its original nurture with a certain indignation. He also knows that the selfhood of every individual person entails a certain biological *donnée*, stubbornly stout and immutable, which is beyond the power of any cultural establishment to manipulate—so that, in his view, there is a dimension of the self which is not, ultimately, at the mercy of culture, and thus some part of our human fate is not bestowed by culture. And Freud's testimony in this regard represents an emphasis with which the author of *Beyond Culture* wants very much, as it were, to cooperate.

Yet Mr. Trilling is by no means prepared to give himself to any simple endorsement of what he calls "the adversary view" of culture. To be sure, he considers it to have sponsored the most creative program in the intellectual and artistic life of the modern period: namely, that program which sought "to liberate the individual from the tyranny of his culture in the environmental sense and to permit him to stand beyond it in an autonomy of perception and judgment." But this program (so vigorously espoused from the late years of the eighteenth century through the first quarter of the present century) has at last now achieved so large a success and has become the property of so populous and influential a class that the pathos of the old legend of the creative minority with its back against the wall, desperately attempting to hold at bay the bullying and powerful bourgeoisie—this pathos no longer seems at all concordant with the actuality of the adversary movement. For in fact its proponents are to be found today not "beyond culture" but in the midst of a new culture, a Second Environment, which "shows the essential traits of any cultural environment: firm presuppositions, received ideas, approved attitudes, and a system of rewards and punishments." The personnel of our universities, of our various public intellectual agencies, of our vast communications industries—all those who make up the great intellectual imperium of contemporary society—are people who are today not without a significant power. And Mr. Trilling wants to remark the degree to which theirs is a class which, as it has grown in size and coherence and influence, has developed its own pieties, its own automatized responses, its own vested interests, and "a considerable efficiency of organization, even of an institutional kind."

So the old pathos, with its theme of the great cost of the adversary commitment, cannot any longer be invoked, in a time when the "adversary culture" has become itself an Establishment, prepotent and self-protective and often nearly indistinguishable from that order which it originally set out to oppose and subvert.

The opening and the concluding essays in *Beyond Culture* record Mr. Trilling's reflections on the teaching of literature today in the university. These discussions mainly concern the conventionalizing of dissent evidenced now by the responses of students to the modern side of the literary curriculum. As he recalls his experience in recent years at Columbia in presenting the great classic canon of modern literature—Yeats and Eliot, Joyce and Kafka, Lawrence and Mann and Gide—he speaks of how quick the young people in his classroom are to engage in a "process we might call the socialization of the anti-social, or the acculturation of the anti-cultural, or the legitimization of the subversive." They take this literature, with all its fierce ambivalence toward the enterprise of civilization, and promptly establish it in "the talkative and attitudinizing" world of the Second Environment, making it the subject of "variations on the accepted formulations about *anxiety*, and *urban society*, and *alienation*, and *Gemeinschaft* and *Gesellschaft*." And the joyous glibness with which they bring to heel a literature that looks into the Abyss and relentlessly harries us with the possibility of damnation, with our consequent obligation to search out the one thing needful—this does indeed make, says Mr. Trilling, a kind of marvel.

In short, an adversary movement which has developed its own orthodoxy, its own cant, its own ground of claim, is no longer the bravely heroic affair that its unthinking (or self-serving) votaries may imagine it still to be; and thus Mr. Trilling wants very carefully to withhold the third cheer. But his deepest misgiving about our modern adversary tradition (qualified, of course, by his profound esteem for its great expressions in the nineteenth and twentieth centuries) pertains to its underlying metaphysic—its Gnosticism, its morbid idealism of unpleasure, the intransigent angelism which prompts it to forsake or to ignore "the actual" and "the conditioned." And, as in *The Opposing Self*, this concern is a shaping consideration in many of the essays in *Beyond Culture*, especially in the brilliant discourse on "Hawthorne in Our Time."

In the journal that he kept during the summer of 1947, when he was taken to Europe to lecture at Harvard's Salzburg Seminar in American Studies, the late F. O. Matthiessen recalled a Finnish girl's asking him one morning at Salzburg what Hawthorne would think of the existentialists. His way of recounting this[10] suggests that he

10F O. Matthiessen, *From the Heart of Europe* (New York: Oxford University Press, 1948), p. 29.

felt it to be a quite natural query, for Matthiessen knew, of course, as he had so amply indicated in *American Renaissance*, how much our way of reading Hawthorne—so different, say, from that of William Crary Brownell and the "genteel tradition"—had been licensed by our great responsiveness to those types of spiritual radicalism in this century in which the existentialists are most deeply implicated. And, in a similar vein, Mr. Trilling is acutely conscious of how insistently *our* Hawthorne represents the human pilgrimage as an uncertain, hazardous journey through a darkly mysterious and threatening world.

Indeed, the darkly negative view of the world expressed in Hawthorne's "romances" strikes Mr. Trilling as closely in accord with that of the writer often thought to bear a relation to our own period much like that which Dante and Goethe bore to theirs: namely, Franz Kafka. For he regards Hawthorne's fiction as determined—in a way not unlike Kafka's—to make only a very minimal reference to the concrete actualities and occasions of human life, since it wants to represent "the world as . . . susceptible to penetration and suffusion by agencies not material and mundane." He proposes that it is just the resulting thinness of his scene that accounts in part for the reserve characterizing the response offered Hawthorne by Henry James (in his famous monograph of 1879)—a reserve, however, emphatically disavowed by the contemporary reader whose great satisfaction with Hawthorne's art derives precisely from the fact of its representing the world as so lacking in thickness and density as to hold forth the possibility of spirit *un*conditioned by circumstance. Yet, says Mr. Trilling,

> it is just here that we are likely to go astray in our perception of Hawthorne. For if it is indeed true that Hawthorne's world is thinly composed, we must yet see

that whatever its composition lacks in thickness is sup-
plied by an iron hardness. There are indeed similarities
to be observed between Kafka and Hawthorne, but
there is—after all, and despite first appearance—this decisive difference between them, that for Hawthorne the
world is always and ineluctably *there* and in a very
stubborn and uncompromising way.

And he means simply that Hawthorne's imagination—in
*The House of the Seven Gables*, in *The Blithedale Romance*, in *The Scarlet Letter* and *The Marble Faun* and the
most typical stories—is always held in strictest accountabil-
ity to "the literal actuality of the world," however much
"the moral life [is represented] as existing beyond the
merely pragmatic, ... as a mystery, as being hidden, dark,
and dangerous, and as having some part of its existence in
a world which is not that of our ordinary knowledge."
Hawthorne was, to be sure, greatly preoccupied by the
ways in which he conceived this world to be open to
ingression from without, from another world. Yet, always,
his concern with *another* world is held under the sway of
his sense of *this* world's intractable tangibility, of "how
often it falls short of being spontaneous, peremptory, and
obligatory." And thus, Mr. Trilling suspects, "the contemporary reader must always ... be somewhat disappointed
by Hawthorne," since that reader—in the degree to which
he is touched by the prevailing pieties of secular spirituality in our time—will be "preoccupied by the ideal of the
autonomous self, or at least of the self as it seeks autonomy in its tortured dream of metaphysical freedom,"
whereas Hawthorne's pieties (though he "could indeed
conceive of our longed-for autonomy") are ultimately
committed elsewhere. For he is an artist of "the conditioned" who "leaves us face to face with the ultimately
unmodifiable world, of which our undifferentiated human

nature is a part"; and, in so far as he is therefore disappointing, he makes simply another measure of the disorientation suffered by the liberal intelligence in the modern period.

*    *    *

Now the polemical ironies which Lionel Trilling over a long period has directed upon the modern passion for the life of "pure spirit" have tended, as was surely expectable, to raise the hackles of many of his literary confreres. As his tone has grown increasingly astringent, the large admiration of his critical work being generally expressed two decades ago after the appearance of *The Liberal Imagination* has in some quarters been withdrawn altogether, or has at least in some quarters been very considerably qualified. The line taken a few years ago by Joseph Frank [11] represents the kind of emphasis that the animadversion has frequently expressed. Mr. Trilling's constant fidgeting over his dialectic of the restlessness of the modern self and the intractability of circumstance, his sharpness toward the great penchant of the liberal imagination for some kind of angelism, his critique of the modern longing for pure spirit, his antipathy toward any impatient rejection of "the conditioned"—all this, says Mr. Frank, simply betokens an opting for "stability and stasis" which, in its disparagement of the will, at best represents a kind of reinstatement of the "inner check" of Irving Babbitt and which, at the worst, represents an intention to substitute "contemplation for an active grappling with social reality." In the late phase of his thought, as he invites us to approve only those

[11]See Joseph Frank, "Lionel Trilling and the Conservative Imagination," *The Widening Gyre: Crisis and Mastery in Modern Literature* (New Brunswick, N.J.: Rutgers University Press, 1963), pp. 253-74.

"forms of being in which the will is absent or quiescent,"
what Mr. Trilling is really about, so the charge goes, is an
elaborate stratagem for endowing "social passivity and
quietism" with an utterly meretricious dignity. And thus,
his aversion to the apocalyptic program having become so
obsessive, he has evolved from an inspiriting "critic of the
liberal imagination . . . into one of the least belligerent and
most persuasive spokesmen of the conservative imagination"—one, indeed, prepared to advocate nothing other
than a "total acceptance" of whatever happens to be the
*status quo* and the here and now. He is, in short, to be
regarded as a reactionary whose chief role today is that of
lending a certain fancy elegance to an essentially obscurantist politics of conformism. It is, indeed, coming from a
critic of Joseph Frank's brilliance, an astonishing estimate;
but it is, nevertheless, the judgment he renders, and—
amidst the general slackening of intellectual life in this
country sponsored in recent years by the devotees of the
New Left—it, even in its drastically simplistic appraisal,
may be far more modulated than the verdict many of the
radical young would now be prepared to hand down.

But surely, in its imputation of a politically reactionary
motive, Mr. Frank's snappishness is by way of prompting
him to lay about so vigorously that his target becomes
virtually unidentifiable with anything intrinsic to the body
of thought with which he is dealing. For the principal
subject of Mr. Trilling's meditation, far from being anything that centrally touches on the public sector of modern life, has most essentially concerned the status of selfhood in a time when the tuition of supernatural religion
appears no longer available and when the most basic prop-
osition of any anthropology seems perforce to be something to the effect of—neither beast nor angel. So, his
procedure being (in his case naturally) to appropriate the
testimony of the literary imagination as the material for a

phenomenology of selfhood, it would seem that he might reasonably expect his readers to consider his work (in the manner in which he speaks in *Beyond Culture* of having encouraged a student in his classroom to think of Mann's *The Magic Mountain*) as having primary "reference . . . to the private life," as touching "the public life only in some indirect or tangential way," and as not therefore justifying its being immediately pounced upon for "a public practicality."

Mr. Trilling is, as we have noticed, at once a man of the Enlightenment (who is thoroughly committed to the adventure of the will, to the rational mastery of the world) and a Romantic (who believes that man is the creature of a world which, ultimately, surpasses his power to weigh and measure and manipulate). His major assumption is what he conceives to have been the inevitable assumption for men living in the West since the time of Rousseau, that our human fate is lived out in relation not to God but to culture, to the ideas and manners distinguishing the social totality that provides the self with its environing matrix of thought and faith and human relationship. In his Preface to *The American*, Henry James speaks of "reality" as "the things we cannot possibly not know," and Mr. Trilling takes it for granted—and not unreasonably—that for the secular intelligence of the modern period the ultimate reality, the thing that cannot possibly not be known, is nothing other than the human polity, the fact of culture itself. With all those who so conceive the nature of ultimacy, he is conscious of sharing a tendency to view culture, however, with a certain indignation, to feel something terrible in the idea of man-in-culture. For it is an idea which holds forth the possibility of man utterly at the mercy of culture; and no thought is more repugnant to modern sensibility than this, since it contravenes the most basic article of any genuinely secular faith—namely, that man has dominion over the world and that the chief instrument of his dominion is reason, free and unfettered and autonomous. So, in its commitment to the dream of autonomy, in its determination not to submit to the coercion of any force other than that of the rational intellect itself, the modern mind has constantly resisted acknowledging the possibility that man might be subject to the conditioning power of any constellation of objective circumstance, even that of culture; and thus it has undertaken to keep faith with its Enlightenment legacy. Yet the insistent testimony in behalf of autonomy has regularly inclined to overreach its intended goal of guaranteeing to man his full human stature, just in the degree to which its denial that he is a beast has proved in effect to be an avowal that he is something like an angel. And it is precisely the unsteadiness of the hold which secular wisdom has kept on the centrist vision—of man as *neither* beast *nor* angel—that has defined for Mr. Trilling his basic problem.

His humanism, in other words, is a very anxious humanism indeed, not because it lacks confidence in its own premises but because it finds the ranks of its own confederacy to be so frequently unreliable, since modern secularity has consistently fumbled its great burden, of upholding the full tension and polarity and modulation that belong to the essential reality of the human. But, for all of his quiet modesty, this is the burden Mr. Trilling has wanted to assume; and thus the focalizing theme of his thought has come to be the nature of the self, at once in its freedom and in its finitude, at once in its autonomy and in its servitude to circumstance. He *is*, in short, John Laskell, for, as he says in *The Opposing Self,* "Only the self that is certain of its existence, of its identity, can do without the armor of systematic certainties."

So, given his concern to speak up for what *The Middle of the Journey* calls "the human being in maturity, at once

responsible and conditioned," and given his concern to
chart out the possibility of a selfhood unreliant upon the
"systematic certainties" of a dogmatic creed (of, as one
supposes, a metaphysical or supernaturalist or political
character), it is not at all surprising that in his most recent
book, *Sincerity and Authenticity* (1972), Mr. Trilling
should finally have been brought round to a consideration
of what indeed the conception of the "authentic" human
life may mean. Yet, here, when he does at last come
immediately before the particular question that the whole
logic of his thought makes necessarily the primary issue for
his engagement, he is very much like the Coleridge of the
*Biographia Literaria*, who, after all his elaborate preparatory maneuvers toward setting forth a doctrine of the
imagination, when he does finally come face to face with
his great problem in the XIIIth Chapter of the *Biographia*,
then, as Basil Willey says, simply "slips lizard-like into a
thicket of learned . . . [circuities], leaving in our hands his
tail only. . . ."[12] But Coleridge's tail, says Professor Willey,
"is not without a sharp point," and so too it is with Mr.
Trilling's: indeed, his may even be said to have at least two
sharp points, these being especially involved in those focal
passages which speak of Hegel and Freud—who would
seem in many ways to be the central figures in his design.

The argument of this most recent book (comprised of
Mr. Trilling's Charles Eliot Norton Lectures at Harvard in
1970) is something much too highly complicated to admit
of any rapid, or even roughly comprehensive, summary;
but suffice it to say that the principal theme of his meditation here concerns the nature and the ground of that
validity of life in which a sober secularity may find human
existence fully effectuated.

[12]Basil Willey, *Nineteenth Century Studies: Coleridge to Matthew
Arnold* (London: Chatto and Windus, 1949), p. 13.

Mr. Trilling is mindful, of course, that the exacting conception of truth in the life of selfhood now embodied in the notion of "authenticity" represents a formulation of the human norm which has only very recently attained its present ascendancy in the moral life. For the older ideal of selfhood was conceived in the terms of that "congruence between avowal and actual feeling" which was called "sincerity." And he considers it altogether natural that in the early modern period—in the sixteenth and seventeenth and eighteenth centuries—men should have stigmatized feigning and dissimulation as strongly as they did. It was a time marked by a great acceleration in the rate of upward social mobility, when the fluid character of life made it newly important that the conduct of affairs be at least predicable upon some steadiness and singleminded fixity in one's neighbor's relation to things and to oneself; and the swiftness with which established communal forms were being revised made it seem equally important that a dynamic social order be submitted to a new kind of critical scrutiny, lest a volatile society become itself a force corruptive of the sincerity of its citizens.

Indeed, under the pressures of an exceedingly variable and shifting culture, the very idea of "society" was, by the last years of the eighteenth century, beginning to seem coextensive with the idea of *in*sincerity. Of this development, Mr. Trilling takes Diderot's famous dialogue *Rameau's Nephew* (composed at some point between 1761 and 1774) to be a crucial document. For the protagonist of the dialogue is one whose presiding attitude toward the social world is one of polemicism. Though himself a prodigiously cultivated musician, he is not a man of genius: so he lives always under the shadow of his celebrated uncle, and the bitterness engendered by the precariousness of his own foothold in the world prompts him to turn a bilious eye on that system of rewards that determines the questions of power and place in society. He considers the entire social drama to be an affair of fraudulence and duplicity, everybody wearing his mask and acting out his role and undertaking to flatter whomever it may be whose good favor is necessary for his own advancement. And the cynicism with which the Nephew does himself proceed systematically to flatter the rich and the powerful is simply an expression of his deepest conviction—that, social reality being what it is, it requires to be dealt with aggressively.

Mr. Trilling is, however, less concerned with the approbation accorded this aggressiveness by Diderot than he is with that which Hegel accorded it. The Diderot of the dialogue is, of course, *un honnête homme* who defends the canons of respectable morality, but the authorial intention controlling the dialogue wants to render a favorable judgment of the Nephew's method of social negotiation, conceiving it to be the only way in which the self can possibly treat with the mercurial and treacherous actuality of social life. But it is not so much in Diderot's own esteem for the Nephew as in that expressed by the Hegel of the *Phenomenology* that Mr. Trilling finds a large paradigm of the modern cultural situation.

Hegel knew the dialogue in Goethe's translation which appeared while he was at work on the *Phenomenology*, and, immediately, its protagonist struck him as splendidly emblematic of what he took to be the modern phase in the development of Spirit. In his plotting of the history of freedom, or of *Geist*, the individual lives initially in a relation of "obedient service" to the body politic, regards it with an "inner reverence," is wholly committed to "the heroism of dumb service," and finds the human norm in the "honest consciousness." But Spirit wants ultimately to be its own master; and thus it is destined by its deep yearning for autonomy eventually to break out of its "dumb service," this being at first so modified, however, as to become not immediately a heroism of revolt but a "heroism of flattery," when the individual, becoming conscious of the contingency of the social covenant, nevertheless continues to support it for prudential reasons. Gradually, however, the "noble" attitude of "dumb service" is replaced by the "base" attitude of open agnosticism with respect to all those principalities and powers that have the effect of suppressing the autonomy of the individual self—though Hegel, of course, expects all partisans of freedom to find in the mien and deportment of the base self an admirable integrity, since it is precisely its baseness, its refusal of obedient service to the external power of society, which permits Spirit to fulfill itself. And it is in fact his own partisanship with the cause of Spirit and its freedom that leads him, in the chapter of the *Phenomenology* that speaks of *Rameau's Nephew,* to reprobate the "honest consciousness" represented by the Diderot of the dialogue and to praise in effect the Nephew for the malice with which he confronts an oppressive society, since it is calculated to raise Spirit to a "higher level of conscious life."

Now it is the same concern for the integrity of the self that kept Hegel from giving his suffrage to the "honest consciousness" which, as Mr. Trilling suggests, has similarly kept many of the great *directeurs de conscience* in the modern period from endorsing the view of the *honnête homme,* of the world as something serious and totally in earnest. Hegel's refusal to cast his vote for an ethic of "sincerity" presents, indeed, a classic prototype of that great refusal which Marx and Nietzsche were also, each in his own way, to encourage. And this is a refusal not simply of the "honest consciousness" but of that basic norm of life which it proposes. For the vision of the ideal condition of the world held by the "honest soul" is one which understands man's felicity to be dependent on certain limiting conditions, of harmony and peace and order and honor—and it is precisely this which the modern mind, as Mr. Trilling understands it, considers to represent an impossible archaicism. On the contrary: the happiest state of affairs is regarded as one in which things are being broken up and disintegrated, and this as a witness to the unconditioned nature of the self. The dream (the old "noble" dream) of man's blessedness as resident in what Joyce called "the fair courts of life," the dream (of Balzac and Flaubert and Trollope and Henry James) that the Good Place is a place of affluent decorum, of what Shakespeare's *The Tempest* speaks of as "quiet days, fair issue, and long life"—this, Mr. Trilling feels, has been largely discredited by the literature of our own period, dominated as it is by what Saul Bellow's *Herzog* calls "the Wasteland outlook":

> It would of course be absurd to say that the present-day repudiation of the old visionary norm controls the lives we actually live. As householders, housekeepers, and parents we maintain allegiance to it in practice, possibly even in diffident principle. But as *readers*, as participants in the conscious, formulating part of our life in society, we incline to the antagonistic position.

For the career of Spirit, it is thought, must not be blocked or retarded, and the ideal condition of the self is believed to be one of liberation from the conditioning power of circumstance. So "the 'honest soul' [is consigned] to the contempt of history."

It is this very defeat which the "honest soul" has suffered in the advanced literature and thought of recent decades that accounts, as Mr. Trilling suspects, for the indifference to Freud which is today represented by the radical young. For the great offense which he now offers is that of his having wanted, indeed, to strengthen the "honest soul," of his having refused the adversary view of society. In his momentous book of 1930, *Civilization and Its Discontents*—which presents his maturest understanding of the relation between mind and society—he does, to be sure, take a tragic view (as he had done in his earlier writings) of the immense psychic costs entailed by social existence, but he does not consider these exactions to be susceptible of any simple mitigation. Always, of course, Freud was preoccupied with a certain intrinsic relationship between social organization and neurosis and would seem to have considered man-in-society to be by definition a neurotic creature, since the mechanisms of collective life necessarily require some repression of those appetitive energies that constitute the essence of the *humanum*. In his sense of the human reality, having neighbors and living one's life in relation to their lives must perforce involve an acceptance of "substitutive gratifications" for certain impulses whose immediate indulgence would be disruptive of the human communion. But the resulting accommodation (for the sake of social order and coherence) of the "pleasure-principle" to the "reality-principle" does, as Freud is at great pains to establish, inevitably entail enormous suffering, because the self, in order to win the advantages offered by civilization, must disown a part of its own inner reality. And it is precisely in the de-authenticization of the self necessitated by the social contract that his psychology locates the mainspring of neurosis. Yet, as Mr. Trilling reminds us, in his great book of 1930 Freud was in effect denying that society is the sufficient cause of our dispeace. For a main burden of *Civilization and Its Discontents* involves his effort to show that it is of the nature of the super-ego, in its fierceness toward the id, by far to exceed anything that the stability of collective life might be conceived to require in the way of the repression of anarchic impulse. Nor does he regard the cruel tyrannousness of the super-ego as easily mitigable by any reordering of societal arrangements. The super-ego does, to be sure, in part originate in the aggressiveness with which the ego maintains (against the id) its contract with the human sodality, but (in Mr. Trilling's summary of Freud's case), "under the mask of a concern with social peace and union, [it] carries on a ceaseless aggression to no purpose save that of the enhancement of its own power ... and, so far from being appeased by acquiescence in its demands, actually increases its severity in the degree that it is obeyed." Its hegemony, in other words, is not established by any logic intrinsic to the nature of society as such; and thus Freud foresees no possibility of any simple alleviation of our profoundest distresses by melioristic schemes of social reconstruction, however valid (for less ultimate reasons) may be the urgency with which conscience enjoins us to support various enterprises of social melioration. The most primal dynamic of the unconscious life, being deeply rooted in the immemorial past of the race, is, in short, simply a given of our human nature whose adverse consequences are incommutable.

Freud's way of thinking, then, is one which *naturalizes* adversity and suffering, as inescapably a part of our human estate: he sees in the deep places of the human soul a kind of hell—and it is there, rather than in any particular pattern of society, that he locates the seat of man's wretchedness. But, as Mr. Trilling suggests, it is just this stern vision of the ultimate mystery and intractability of our basic woe which in the world of contemporary radical thought is felt to be an intolerable affront. For the new wise men, whether in the manner of a Michel Foucault or an R. D. Laing or a Norman Brown, are convinced that *in*authenticity is simply consequent upon the pressures exerted on the individual by a restrictive society. So much, in fact, is inculpation of social reality the controlling category of their thought that they are even inclined, increasingly, to de-

clare that in madness alone is there to be found an appropriate way of dealing with the tyrannous inauthenticity
of the social world, that in madness alone do we find a
form of life that deserves to be adjudged humanly authentic. Indeed, in Mr. Trilling's by no means implausible
estimate, "a consequential part of the educated public"
today, in its enthrallment by one or another kind of
ecstatic antinomianism, finds it

> . . . gratifying to entertain the thought that alienation is
> to be overcome only by the completeness of alienation,
> and that alienation completed is not a deprivation or
> deficiency but a potency. Perhaps exactly because the
> thought is assented to so facilely, so without what used
> to be called seriousness, it might seem that no expres-
> sion of disaffection from social existence was ever so
> desperate as this eagerness to say that authenticity of
> personal being is achieved through an ultimate isolate-
> ness and through the power that this is presumed to
> bring—the falsities of an alienated social reality rejected
> in favor of an upward psychopathic mobility to the
> point of divinity, each one of us a Christ but with none
> of the inconveniences of interceding, of being a sacri-
> fice, of reasoning with rabbis, of making sermons, of
> having disciples, of going to weddings and to funerals, of
> beginning something and at a certain point remarking
> that it is finished.

Thus it is now, in our own late time, that the modern
passion for the life of pure spirit is, *in extremis*, to be
found to be a passion for madness.

\*     \*     \*

Here, then, are the main lines of the inquiry into the
literary and intellectual climate of our time that Lionel
Trilling over the past generation has kept steadily in prog-

ress, and it will doubtless generally be felt by those who have closely followed his course that he is a very strict arbiter indeed. In the famous opening paragraph of his essay on "The Function of Criticism at the Present Time," Matthew Arnold (in repetition of a passage from his earlier lectures "On Translating Homer") declared the "critical effort" necessarily to be "the endeavor . . . to see the object as in itself it really is." And in this most essential particular, as in much else, Mr. Trilling throughout his career has remained a dedicated Arnoldian. But, earlier on, I suggested that his primary métier in many respects may be thought of as having been that of "anthropology," for the object which above all others he has wanted to see as in itself it really is has been nothing other than the human fact, the creature who is man, in his full human stature. And, against most of his brethren in the corridors of secular intellectual life, he has felt obliged to say, again, what Arnold wanted to say of the English Romantics, that, though having "plenty of energy, plenty of creative force, [they do] . . . not *know* enough." Which is to say, so far as Mr. Trilling is concerned, that, with but a few exceptions, the best secular wisdom in the modern period has failed, in any impressive way, to hold consistently to the kind of sanity that Western humanism in its greatest moments has realized, that man (as Pascal says in the 358th Fragment of the *Pensées*) "is neither angel nor brute." But on no occasion, of course, has he consented to confront any of the great religious geniuses of the tradition: for all of his wide-ranging culture, Augustine and Pascal, Kierkegaard and Barth, Tillich and Niebuhr are quite as if they had never been: so confirmed is he in the prejudices of a man of the Enlightenment that not even, as a Jew, does he pay any attention, say, to a Moses Hess or a Franz Rosenzweig, to a Martin Buber or an Abraham Heschel. So, since it is alone the central modern traditions of secular thought to which Mr. Trilling chooses to address himself and since, in his sense of things, there, the centrist vision has more often than not been abrogated, his procedure, inevitably, seems in a strange way to be like that of the great theological doctors of the Negative Way: it often appears primarily to involve the method of aposiopesis, of saying (against the Modern Anthology)—"Not that ... and not that ... and not that. ..."

Yet, if the definition of man as *neither* beast *nor* angel is not itself to make for a kind of weightlessness that robs the human reality of any radical seriousness, the question being raised in the 427th Fragment of the *Pensées* must finally be faced—namely, in what rank, then, *is* man to be placed. "He has plainly gone astray," says Pascal, "and fallen from his true place without being able to find it again. He seeks it anxiously and unsuccessfully everywhere in impenetrable darkness." But where *ought* he to turn, and what *is* the nature of his "place"? The question needs to be posed, one feels, with something like the bluntness of those anxious metaphysical queries that a college sophomore flings out at the world—so persistently do Mr. Trilling's characteristic strategems simply subtilize his central problem into a matter disposable by a graceful pirouette of rhetoric.

It is, indeed, a measure of Mr. Trilling's special sort of greatness that, after Coleridge, he is one of the very few literary critics of the modern period whose basic endeavor is of such a kind as to ask for completion by some large and genuinely constructive philosophical effort. And the gingerliness with which he has skirted this final aspect of his enterprise makes for the special sort of disappointment which his work calls forth.

It may well be, of course, that this is an inadvertence which, at least over a long span of time, was to be accounted for in the terms of Mr. Trilling's Arnoldian commitment. In his book on Arnold, it is true, he sheered away from that side of Arnold's thought which proposes that, given the collapse of dogmatic religion in the modern world, literature itself must now be assigned the decisive kerygmatic task, of (as Arnold said in his essay on "The Study of Poetry") interpreting life for us, of consoling us, and sustaining us. But though, when he was preparing this book in the 1930s, Mr. Trilling clearly foresaw many of the embarrassments that must overtake us when we ask literature to become a surrogate for religion,[13] in many of the crucial statements in *The Liberal Imagination*, as it sometimes seemed, literature was being regarded as the one thing needful. For there we were told that the special capacity of literature (particularly of the novel) is for "the perception of the dangers of the moral life": it is, so the argument went, "the most effective agent of the moral imagination" in the modern period and the great guarantor of "moral realism," its most important work being "the work of reconstituting and renovating the will." And it is no doubt the very explicit identification of the moral with the aesthetic in his book of 1950 that has led one of Mr. Trilling's critics to charge that his thought is touched in no small degree by what requires to be denominated simply as aestheticism.[14] Yet, even in *The Liberal Imagination*, he was sufficiently uneasy about such a commitment as to remark (in his essay on "Art and Fortune") that, just as "the over-valuation of love is the beginning of the end of love," so too may "the over-valuation of art . . . [be] the beginning of the end of art." By the midsixties he had, indeed, come to the point of believing (as he says in the Preface to *Beyond Culture*) that art may "not always tell

---

[13]Trilling, *Matthew Arnold*, rev. ed., pp. 374-80.
[14]See Mark L. Krupnick, "Lionel Trilling: Criticism and Illusion," *Modern Occasions*, 1, no. 2 (Winter, 1971): 282-87.

the truth or the best kind of truth and . . . [may] not
always point out the right way, that it . . . [may] even
generate falsehood and habituate us to it, and that, on
frequent occasions, it . . . [may, therefore, be necessary
to] subject [it] . . . to the scrutiny of the rational intellect." And in his most recent book, *Sincerity and Authenticity*, though he is not wholly comfortable with the
extreme insistence on the positively corruptive power of
the arts expressed by Rousseau (in his so-called *First
Discourse* and in his *Letter to M. d'Alembert on the
Theatre*), he is yet inclined to grant a considerable cogency
to Rousseau's claim that the arts, far from fostering the
autonomy of the self, are in fact an agent of conformism.
For he feels that, in our own time, when they have so
much become a property of the Second Environment,
instead of offering a man a "smithy in which to forge his
autonomous selfhood," they may afford little more than
simply another field of gossip and received opinion.

So what has apparently been the tendency of Mr. Trilling's thought in recent years, to set aside his earlier Arnoldian faith in the redemptive power of art, may augur
some new readiness to undertake in a more forthright way
the further philosophical (and perhaps even in some sense
theological) task of which it has been the special distinction of his literary criticism to be a kind of pledge. At least
this, one feels, is the best hope to be entertained for the
remaining phase of his career. For, very probably, it will
not be until aposiopesis as the method of his cultural
criticism begins to be replaced by some more positively
assertory mode which is rooted in a developed philosophical anthropology that Mr. Trilling will finally be released,
particularly by many of his younger readers today, from
the suspicion that his thought ultimately lines itself up
behind nothing more than a stasis of the given. And this,
one suspects, is indeed the impression it very often con-

veys now to the populous younger public which wants to say, with that proprietor of a London pub in *The Waste Land*, "HURRY UP PLEASE ITS TIME." Against the reductionism and the rationalism and the angelism of the modern intelligence, Mr. Trilling's concern to make the centrist testimony (neither beast nor angel) has required him, again and again, to say, "Not that . . . and not that. . . ." But to the New Sensibility the sum of his negatives, with all their solicitude for the tensions and balances within extremes, may perhaps seem only a very unheroic shoring up of things as they are. And, furthermore, it may be felt that his way of counterposing "this world in its ordinary actuality," with its daily rituals of keeping the hearth, against that rejection of the quotidian to which we are invited by the angelic mind, that this plangent elevation of the "securities of bourgeois routine"[15] adds up only to the New Philistinism. In his own prevision of so unjust a verdict, Mr. Trilling, with a touch of exasperation, has remarked (in *The Opposing Self*) that he has no wish "to speak . . . against the sense of urgency or immediacy, or against power or passion," that he does not take what Wordsworth called "the sentiment of Being" to be "the whole desideratum of the emotional life"—and I am persuaded that he has no such inclination. But, surely, if he is to be a more persuasive and a more useful adversary of "the tigers of wrath," it is necessary for him to present, in a truly systematic way, a case the articles of which, in the nature of the affair, must extend beyond the considerations of literary criticism.

Perhaps the one suggestion of this necessity which it will be sufficiently illustrative to cite is the curiously enigmatic use he makes of the concept of "biology." I have already remarked the happy welcome he gives to that phase of

15*Ibid.*, p. 285.

Freud's thought which wants to "establish the self beyond the reach of culture," which wants to testify to a dimension of man's humanity that surpasses any power of control or coercion that may be exercised by the agencies of society and politics. This is an emphasis in Freud's system which Mr. Trilling himself wants most heartily to endorse. And it is, indeed, his own insistence on this theme which ought to be unsettling for those hostile critics of his thought who tax him with an inclination to quietism and social passivity, for in the notion of a stoutness and integrity at the core of human selfhood that are beyond the reach of cultural control there is surely implicit a radical principle of judgment wherewith any and every *status quo* may be submitted to a very stringent test. But what is puzzling is that Mr. Trilling should regularly speak (in *The Opposing Self*, in *Beyond Culture*, in *Sincerity and Authenticity*) of this "hard, irreducible, stubborn core" of selfhood which is "beyond the reach of culture" as a *biological* fact. "It seems to me," he says (in the essay on Freud in *Beyond Culture*), "that whenever we become aware of how entirely we are involved in our culture and how entirely controlled by it we believe ourselves to be, destined and fated and foreordained by it, there must come to us a certain sense of liberation when we remember our biological selves." And he even suggests that when a people, "living under imposed conditions of a very bad kind," yet manage, with however many psychic scars, to survive with their human dignity still intact, it is because they cannot finally be robbed of some sense of themselves as "biological facts." Now this, one feels, represents not simply an eccentric use of language but a real confusion of thought. For, as Mr. Trilling might be reminded by thinkers so diverse as Miguel de Unamuno and Jean-Paul Sartre, Max Scheler and Reinhold Niebuhr, Martin Buber and Karl Jaspers, men are empowered to perform the act of self-definition in trans-cultural terms by their freedom—and thus it is not a *biological* but a *spiritual* fact which gives them some vantage ground above and beyond the reach of culture. Their capacity for transcendence with respect to any system of social and political cohesion is, in short, simply misconceived if taken to be a fact of *nature* rather than a fact of *spirit;* and it can only be concluded that the strangely inapt language with which Mr. Trilling deals with the issues of freedom and transcendence is but an indication of the need for his thought to seek a very much greater systematic clarity, as it moves out beyond the field of literary aesthetics and criticism into the region of philosophical anthropology.

Yet it is to be hoped that the making of this kind of notation may not in itself entail that failure in tact responsible for one of the besetting sins of American intellectual life today: namely, the sin of ingratitude. For, whatever may be the unresolved ambiguities in the work that Lionel Trilling has produced, our strongest sense of his achievement ought surely to be of the richness it has *added* to the life of the mind in this country over the past generation and of the cause that we have, therefore, for thinking of it primarily in the terms of gratitude. He does himself (in *Beyond Culture*) attribute to W. H. Auden the remark that great books are not simply read, that they do in turn read us as well. And so it might also be said of him, that he is one of the Americans of our time whom we have read but by whom we have ourselves been far more deeply read— which is perhaps to say that, whatever may be the proper estimate of his limitations, he still remains a part of the best we have.

# Afterword

# V

# Afterword

One of the most remarkable passages in Jean-Paul Sartre's great book of 1943, *Being and Nothingness,* is that which he devotes to an extended meditation on the problem of "the Other"—and it makes, indeed, a very large parable of the modern situation. He considers the distinctively human world to be everywhere marked by alienation and conflict. For, as he reasons, one does not begin to exist in any truly living way for another person until one is *looked* at, and one's neighbor in turn does not himself begin to enter one's own field of attention until he is *seen:* he and I are by way of becoming fellowmen, in other words, only when he looks at me and I look at him. But "the look," as Sartre reminds us, is a profoundly ambiguous and even menacing thing, since, once I begin to "gaze" at my neighbor, he becomes "the Other": he becomes a sort of object—which is to say that, in so far as he exists only as one who is being looked at, he is to that extent at the mercy of a freedom which is not his own. So the moment in which another's look is directed upon me is the moment in which I am at the point of becoming a slave; and, similarly, no sooner do I begin to gaze at my neighbor than his freedom begins to be diminished, for now his human presence begins to be an affair not of his own freedom but of mine. Indeed, in Sartre's account, the human drama is forever one of competing egos struggling to maintain their respective identities against the disintegrative threat of the "look" or "gaze." For, if I am not looking at someone else and thus putting his freedom in jeopardy, he is looking at me and thus threatening mine, so that always and everywhere we dwell in a state of instability in relation to the Other—which is a condition so excruciating as to prompt one of the characters in Sartre's play *No Exit* to utter the famous line, "Hell—is others."

Now this *psychanalyse existentielle* does, of course, in its insistence upon the ultimate inaccessibility and ominousness of the Other, project a distinctively modern sort of vision, and one which—(with diverse variations) in Rousseau and Byron, in Stendhal and Baudelaire, in Schopenhauer and Nietzsche—became irresistible, once man's center of gravity, being no longer found in his relationship with God, began inevitably to be relocated amidst his relations with his fellowmen and the things and processes of nature and history. In his little book of 1843 called *Repetition*, Kierkegaard says: "One sticks one's finger into the soil to tell by the smell in what land one is." But then a certain moment arrived in the early modern period when, after having stuck one's finger into existence, one smelt nothing at all—whereupon the great questions became:

> Where am I? Who am I? How came I here? What is this thing called the world? . . . . Who is it that has lured me into the thing, and now leaves me? Who am I? . . . . How did I obtain an interest in this big enterprise they call reality? Why should I have an interest in it?[1]

---

[1]Sören Kierkegaard, *Repetition: An Essay in Experimental Psychology*, trans. Walter Lowrie (Princeton: Princeton University Press, 1941), p. 114.

Which is to say that once the linchpin of human existence could no longer easily be located in the dimension of Transcendence, the category of what Kierkegaard denominated the "single one" had surely then to become the definitive category of man's self-interpretation. The environing reality of the human enterprise was now, as it seemed, nothing other than the web of political and cultural circumstance—into which man had simply been "thrown." And it was this new sense of *Geworfenheit*, of having been hurled into a world not of our making, that installed at the center of modern consciousness the question of the "single one" or what we now customarily speak of as the problem of the self. When, in other words, the human individual comes to be thought of as surrounded simply by Others—by the Philistines, or the Masses, or the Crowd—the great issue is then felt to be that of how the self may be kept from being altogether overwhelmed by Society or by Culture. The most sensitive men begin to feel (as André Malraux remarked in his Preface to *Days of Wrath*) that "It is difficult to be a man," for, amidst all the tangled collectivities of politics and culture that encircle and press in upon our lives, wherein can it be said that our human career is truly *ours*? Thus it is that, in a time of the eclipse of God, the most characteristic form of the religious question becomes the question of authenticity, of how we are to keep faith with and safeguard the "single one" or the "true self"—in a bullying world.

It is just here, indeed—in the distinctively modern question of authenticity—that we may locate the ground whereon the meeting occurs between the three Americans to whom the essays making up this book are devoted, Norman Mailer and Saul Bellow and Lionel Trilling. I have spoken of them as moralists—which may seem a loose usage of the term, for *Webster's New International Dictionary of the English Language* tells us that a moralist is "one who moralizes; a teacher or student of morals; a writer seeking to inculcate moral duties." They are, of course, all three, students of morals—not primarily, to be sure, in the sense of ideals but of the actualities of human behavior. Yet none seeks in any simple way to "moralize" or "to inculcate moral duties," and Mr. Bellow, in recording his belief that today we suffer from a surfeit of "wise counsel and good precept," thereby very clearly forswears any intention himself to be a moralizer. But in the large, informal meaning we give the term today these three are yet moralists, for, though not systematic thinkers, they, each in his own way, have produced a "literature [which] wishes to give the sensations and to win the responses that are given and won by ideas. . . ."[2] Furthermore, they are profoundly committed to that project Matthew Arnold called the "criticism of life": which is to say that they want to cross-question us into a deeper understanding of the way we live now, and each wants to make a statement—in part admonitory, in part emboldening—about what the jargon of the age names the Human Condition.

Nor is the epithet that has been applied to Mr. Trilling to be reserved for him alone, for Saul Bellow and Norman Mailer equally represent a very "anxious" sort of humanism—which is what makes them (in an Emersonian way) "representative men." For them the central human reality of our time is that of the embattled self, what Mr. Trilling calls "the opposing self." And both Saul Bellow and Norman Mailer would endorse Mr. Trilling's sense of the appositeness of Hegel's remark about the principle of culture being a *terrible* principle, for this is what they take the self to be needing to fend off—namely, the terrible

[2]Lionel Trilling, *The Liberal Imagination* (New York: Viking Press, 1950), p. 289.

potency of the ideas and attitudes and systems of life that constitute the otherness represented by the vast collectives in which modern men dwell.

"The inculpation of society," says Mr. Trilling, "has become with us virtually a category of thought." And, indeed, as we have noticed, the kind of intelligence expressing itself in the careers of Norman Mailer and Saul Bellow and Lionel Trilling does, in its dealings with the social-cultural realities of our period, take a decidedly polemical direction. Their targets are differently defined: with Mailer and Bellow, it is (to paraphrase a passage in *Augie March*) everything in American life that seeks to keep the individual person from having "a charge counter to the central magnetic one" and from dancing "his own dance on the periphery"; whereas, with Trilling, in recent years it has increasingly become what he calls the *second* environment (of "the adversary culture") which, in its automatization of the gestures of protest, loses any real spiritual advantage over the *first* and becomes itself a kind of jail. And, of course, their styles are different: Bellow's very often is that of the gay lampoonist, Mailer's that of the voluble and adroit *enragé* specializing in the *vita activa*, and Trilling's that of the learned patrician looking out upon the "darkling plain,/Swept with confused alarms of struggle and flight." But all three are adepts in the inculpation of those powers and principalities in our cultural life today which bruise and attenuate the life of the self.

Yet, finally—and this is what chiefly makes them exemplary figures on the American scene of the present time—it is not inculpation which is the controlling category of their thought, and (like Bellow's Moses Herzog) they refuse to "live a disappointed life." Each knows how oppressive, in the terms of ideology and politics, the world of Others can be—that "vast public life," as Bellow calls it, which "drives private life into hiding."[3] And none wants to give his suffrage to those dehumanizing systems of bureaucratic rationality which, in Mailer's mythography, bear the name of Totalitarianism. Yet each knows that the world supports and confirms the sacrament of selfhood only in the degree to which it is organized along the lines of some viable form of coexistence. Bellow, for example, is careful to see to it that Moses Herzog is finally brought to the point of discovering that " 'Man liveth not by Self alone but in his brother's face' "—just as Mr. Sammler at last is made to discern that there is no life outside the terms of our "contract" with our fellowmen. Even Mailer, for all his frequent journeys along the dark underside of things, remains finally a dedicated megalopolitan whose ventures into the murkiness of "existentialist" metaphysics are but a way of designing (in Auden's phrase) "new styles of architecture" for the actual streets of the actual *Polis*, and he has lately been indicating in numerous ways his intention not to be "too compulsively ready for the apocalyptic."[4] In short, these are men who, despite their differences of style, share a common scepticism about the pertinence to "the ordinary universe" of what Mr. Trilling disdainfully speaks of (in *The Opposing Self*) as "the demand for life as pure spirit." And thus—quite apart from the particular respects in which they may happen to be wrong about this or about that—they are men whose testimony can have the effect of recommitting us to the common tasks of the human City, in (to use Buber's phrase) this "radically demanding historical hour." Indeed,

---

[3]Saul Bellow, *Recent American Fiction*—A Lecture Presented under the Auspices of the Gertrude Clarke Whittall Poetry and Lecture Fund (Washington, D. C.: The Library of Congress, 1963), p. 2.

[4]Norman Mailer, *The Prisoner of Sex* (Boston: Little, Brown, 1971), p. 204.

they are (as Richard Poirier has remarked of Mailer and Trilling) men "personally gauged, chastened, and disciplined by acutely temperamental involvements with the historical forces they write about."[5] So, being thus chastened, they do not conceive it to be a useful thing to represent human life as an affair of shipwreck on an empty sea, with 70,000 fathoms of water our sole support. They want rather to say, "Fare forward. . . ."

[5]Richard Poirier, *The Performing Self* (New York: Oxford University Press, 1971), p. 179.

## Bibliographical Note

The Introduction incorporates a small segment of my essay, " 'New Heav'ns, New Earth'—the Landscape of Contemporary Apocalypse," which was first published in the University of Chicago's *Journal of Religion*, Vol. 53, No. 1 (January, 1973). And the chapter on Saul Bellow is a revised and very considerably expanded version of an essay first published (under the title "*Sola Gratia*—the Principle of Bellow's Fiction") in *Adversity and Grace: Studies in Recent American Literature*, ed. by Nathan A. Scott, Jr. (Chicago: University of Chicago Press, 1968). The original materials are included here with the permission of the University of Chicago Press.

The chapter on Lionel Trilling formed the basis of the Turnbull Lecture at the Johns Hopkins University, delivered in March of 1973.

# Index